Make Space Make Symbols

A Personal Journey Into Prayer

Keith Clark, Capuchin

Ave Maria Press · Notre Dame, Indiana 46556

To those who have shared their lives with me
and who, by so doing,
have been my teachers in prayer;
and to Marlene
who gave the workshop
which provided the leisure
which allowed the thoughts
to find words.

© 1979 by Ave Maria Press, Notre Dame, Indiana 46556

All rights reserved. No portion of this book may be reproduced
in any form without the written permission of the publisher.

Library of Congress Catalog Card Number: 78-73826

International Standard Book Number: (Cloth) 0-87793-172-0
                                    (Paper) 0-87793-173-9

Art by Joyce Stanley

Manufactured in the United States of America.

Contents

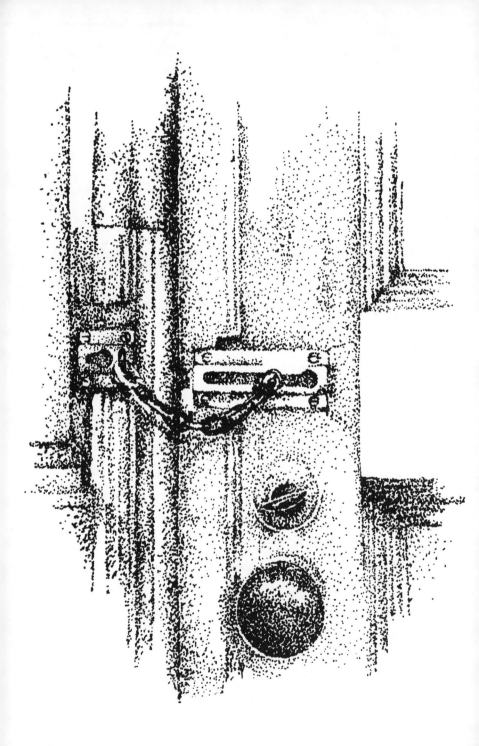

Preface

I began writing this book with a feeling that it was foolish of me even to begin. But I wanted to write a book on prayer.

I think I have a talent for teaching about prayer. I'm not sure I'm good at teaching people to pray, but I can teach them about prayer. If they want to pray, they might benefit from what I can tell them about the project they are undertaking.

For years I've talked about writing a book, but it always seemed like something other people did, not something I would do. I started writing once, but gave it up after I had struggled with the first chapter.

During the past year, however, I have been keeping a record of my thoughts and reactions to things. I hesitate to call what I've been doing a journal; "journal" seems too formal a word. I have simply recorded my thoughts almost daily in a series of spiral notebooks—my green book. So this time when I sat down to write I could reclaim many of my previous thoughts and ideas and feelings.

There are so many books on prayer that I have the feeling that I have to justify, to myself at least, putting another one on the market. I've read several books written by other people; I've benefited from what they wrote. I'm writing for those who, like me, know deep in their hearts that prayer is a profound, satisfying, pleasant and necessary part of life, and something which makes good sense, but who, like me, don't always experience it that way.

Others have helped me by what they've written, and I hope someone will profit from what I've done.

—Keith Clark

Introduction

The title of this book is inspired by the passage from the book of Revelation in which John is instructed to write to the Church at Laodicea (Rev 3:14 ff.). Here is the letter he was told to write:

> The Amen, the faithful Witness and true, the Source of God's creation, has this to say: I know your deeds; I know you are neither hot nor cold. How I wish you were one or the other —hot or cold! But because you are lukewarm, neither hot nor cold, I will spew you out of my mouth! You keep saying, "I am so rich and secure that I want for nothing." Little do you recognize how wretched you are, how pitiably poor and blind and naked! Take my advice. Buy from me gold refined by fire if you would be truly rich. Buy white garments in which to be clothed, if the shame of your nakedness is to be covered. Buy ointment to smear on your eyes, if you would see once more. Whoever is dear to me I reprove and chastise. Be earnest about it, therefore. Repent!
>
> Here I stand, knocking at the door. If anyone hears me calling and opens the door, I will enter his house and have supper with him, and he with me.

The risen Lord who is alive and among his churches has a message for the people in Laodicea who believe in him. He says they are bad, unacceptable to him. They are neither hot nor cold. Jesus isn't asking that they be really good or really bad; he's asking that they be really good. We like our coffee or tea hot and we like our beer cold. Hot is good; cold is good. But when we get wound up in our conversations over coffee in the morning or over our beer in the evening, and just before we go back to work or off to bed we take that last swallow of coffee or beer, it's pretty putrid! It's lukewarm, and that's bad.

So, Jesus says he wishes that the people at Laodicea were good, not bad. But because they've gone bad, he's about to spit them out of his mouth.

And here's what made them bad: they had developed some false hopes and shaky reliances. "You keep saying, 'I am so rich and secure that I want for nothing.' "

Such an easy mistake for Laodicea! They had a gold refinery there, and were proud of the quality of their gold. They also made woolen cloth, and it was a pretty good quality of wool cloth—it bleached almost white. And they made an ointment for the eyes there, and exported it to other towns. They were secure in what they were able to do.

But Jesus warns them that they are poor—a surprising thing to say to a city which refined gold. And they are blind—with all that eye ointment. And they who made cloth were naked.

They had gone bad because they had come to rely on their own efforts and achievements. Jesus invites them to come to him to get the cloth they need to cover their shameful nakedness; to come to him to get the ointment which will cure their blindness. Their own gold had made them poor; their own cloth had left them naked; their own ointment had made them blind. They had become self-sufficient.

It was an easy mistake for the people of Laodicea,

and it's an easy mistake for almost everyone today. Few
people want for anything essential. And that makes re-
liance on the risen Lord almost artificial. Until we see
that our riches make us poor and our decorations and
frills make us naked and our wisdom makes us blind, we
will not easily turn to the Lord. So he warns us, because
he cares for us: "Whoever is dear to me I reprove and
chastise. Be earnest about it, therefore. Repent!"

The false sense of security is particularly bad when it
seeps from our economic life into our religious existence.
For those who were raised in an atmosphere of prayer and
worship, the temptation to feel secure in accustomed religious practices can be almost irresistible—for a while.
But eventually those practices can become meaningless and
may be abandoned. That's sad, perhaps, but it is also the
first step toward "being earnest," toward "repenting." The
first step toward rediscovering prayer.

Taking up serious praying again—or for the first
time—seems to be a complicated and mysterious undertaking. It can seem like trying to make a long-distance
phone call after a winter ice storm. Are the lines still up?
Are the circuits so crowded that there is no way to get my
call in? Do I have the number right? Will the phone ring?
Will anyone be home? Will he answer the phone? Will
he want to talk with me? Is it worth trying at all? Or
should I just forget about it until later? Maybe this isn't
the right time to bother him—or to be bothered by the
inclination I have to call.

Prayer can seem to be an attempt to establish contact with an absent God through a complicated and intri-
cate process with which I am only vaguely familiar. But
Jesus tells us that this is not the case; as a matter of fact,
the opposite is true. Prayer is his attempt to reach us and
it involves our openness and availability to be reached.

"Here I stand, knocking at the door," he says. "If
anyone hears me calling and opens the door, I will come
in and share a meal with him, and he with me."

Sharing a meal is an expression of intimacy. If you and a friend have only one loaf of bread, and that is the only food you have for the day; and if your life is sustained only by that half a loaf of bread which you ate, and your friend's life is sustained by the other half of that same loaf, you are both alive only because of that one loaf. Sharing the loaf or the meal is the establishing of intimacy so deep that lives are actually one.

Jesus' offer of intimacy is very free. His offer isn't even that we should come to him; it is that he comes to us. But it is nonetheless dependent on our receiving him: "If anyone hears me calling and opens the door. . . ." That's not always easy.

If we are going to hear him knocking, we will have to *make space* amid the clutter and clatter of our lives. A knock at our door won't be heard if the din within is all-consuming of our attention. Making space means to be quiet—not just the kind of quiet that comes from removing sounds which beat against our eardrums. It means stilling the noise of our own thoughts and concerns and pre-occupations. But it starts by removing the external noise.

Making space means to be alone—to be free even from the temptation to measure up to the expectations of the people around me. It means clearing the land where I want to sink my roots. It means being enough by myself that the opinions and preferences of others need not manipulate me now. Later they may again dominate me, but not now. Shakespeare said, "All the world's a stage"; and we live most of our lives on that stage, playing a role, in costume, be-hind makeup. Making space is getting off that stage, getting out of the costume, laying aside the script, and tak-ing off the paint; it's retiring to the dressing room alone.

Making space means to take time. It means sitting still long enough to run out of things to think about and to say. I can be alone and quiet and, when that is achieved, I may congratulate myself and break off my prayer. That's a mistake. It's hurrying too much. At that point I'm just getting ready to pray, not finished praying. Leisure is necessary in order to find space—to make space. Those who make space *will* hear him knocking. If you are alone and quiet long enough, you will hear the knocking. When the knock is heard, there remains but to open the door. Again that sounds easy—and in a certain sense it is. But for lots of reasons it can be difficult to do that very easy thing. Most of us want to tidy up the house before we open the door for the visitor. We want to clear the table, to make the bed, to straighten up the room— or at the very least we want to glance around to see that everything is acceptable before we admit him to our lifespace. And, of course, we never feel like everything is acceptable.

To open the door to admit him requires that we *make symbols* expressive of who and how we are. All prayer is our attempt to make ourselves available to him. Prayer is not going in search of God; it is seeking to be found by him. It is making ourselves available to him. It is opening the door to let him in to ourselves—ourselves as we really are.

There are all sorts of religious symbols we can make. Many of them are borrowed from other people or from great religious traditions. Words are symbols. Gestures and postures are symbols. Clothing is a symbol. We know a lot of symbols; the trick is to choose or to make the symbol which expresses me as I really am. I can choose or make words which express me as I really am, or I can choose or make words which are expressive of how I ought to be, or how I think I ought to be, or how I think he thinks I ought to be. And that's a mistake. For prayer to be real, and for prayer to be really my prayer, I have to open the door to let him in to me as *I really am!* Sometimes that's difficult. I may hear him knocking and want to let him in, but I tell myself that first I have to tidy up a bit. I want to repent in private; then I'll let him in!

I've come to believe that authentic prayer consists of

making myself available to God to be touched and moved by him. I do this by making space to hear him knocking and by making symbols which open the door to him. I may indeed choose symbols from great religious traditions, but they are great religious traditions precisely because they are expressive of humankind's eternally valid stances before God. Insofar as I know those symbols to be expressive of me, they are mine to use. But I can also make my own symbols, symbols which no one else ever made. He is knocking at *my* door and seeks entry into *my* life.

The fact that you are even inclined to pick up a book about praying probably indicates that you've already heard him knocking. No one can even desire to pray unless the Lord inspires the inclination. If you would take up prayer seriously, make space, make symbols! That's what this book is about.

1. Clearing the Land
—Space Outside

From August of 1968 until August of 1975 I lived in a large friary on 30 acres of land in rural Indiana. The lawn in front of the friary was large and landscaped. On one side of the house was a woods—domesticated by lawn mower and some attempt to regulate the paths through the trees. Behind the house was an apple orchard.

My job while I was there demanded that I be on duty almost all day and until late in the evening. It was simply a matter of being available to the young men who were novices in our order, to our neighbors and to the people in town. I had classes to prepare and teach during the day, in addition to confessions for sisters, talks to various groups, some counseling—activities which just seemed to demand my time. And I enjoyed it.

After I had been there two years I was appointed the guardian (superior) of the men in the house. I felt embarrassed about that. I wasn't sure that I could be what they needed or wanted. Yet, after my appointment I wanted to promise them that I would try to carry out my new duties as spiritual leader of the group. But I didn't even know what to promise.

I never did make any promises to them; but I promised myself I would spend an hour each day alone. That continued to be difficult; I couldn't find a time when I was not in danger of being interrupted.

Eventually I got into the habit of saying good-night about 11:30 each night. Everyone supposed I was going to bed, so they didn't expect me to be available anymore that day. But I didn't go to bed; I went for a walk. And during the last half hour of that day and the first half hour of the new day I walked through the woods and the orchard. I didn't go out there to pray, nor to think, but simply to walk—to be alone. It became my space—alone and quiet for an hour.

During those walks I did a lot of thinking and worrying and even some praying. In the spring and summer and even quite late into the fall, it was usually a pleasant experience to walk there. When it rained, I could walk under the covered archway in back of the house. Winter posed a problem, but still I walked virtually every night.

I got to know this space very well. I began to follow the paths through the woods without my eyes having to strain to see where I would set my foot on the path; my feet seemed to pick out the route without my paying any attention. I got to know the trees quite personally. They all seemed to pray—each in its own way. Some were nervous and quivering in their prayer. Some looked depressed. There were a few young trees whose prayer was fledgling prayer . . . but they prayed. The pine trees prayed together in their rows. The oak trees seemed uninspired, but they continued to pray.

One tree on the property was taller than all the rest. It was a cottonwood tree. It divided into three separate straight trunks almost immediately after it grew out of the ground, and each part of that tree reached higher into the sky than the four-story friary I could see in the distance. It had dignity. Its prayer was dignified. It prayed in a way I knew I never could. Its waxy leaves on their thin stems always clattered against one another. Even on what seemed like a perfectly still summer night, the cottonwood still murmured its prayer. It was faithful to prayer.

That was my space—a place where I could be alone and quiet for a long time. I loved it. In looking for the place in which to create my space outside myself, I looked for places where I could be alone so that whatever symbols I might make could flow from me uninhibitedly, no matter how outrageous or how tender or how silly or profound. I needed a place where I could be me.

Four years passed, and each turn of the season renewed my enchantment with that place and the space it provided for prayer. Walking out the back door into the orchard almost immediately calmed my spirit. The space outside myself helped create space within. And I could hear the Lord knocking.

I passed well into my 30s during those years, and even began to feel a little bit like I was aging. I began to dislike the coming of winter. Going to my space outside was not very inviting in the winter. Late one fall I said to Mike, one of the young men I lived with, "I don't care to see winter come this year. It makes going outside to my space more difficult." After a short pause Mike said, "I'm sure a man of your intelligence has found an alternative for the winter months."

Well, the simple fact was that I hadn't even thought to look for an alternative. I didn't tell him that, but I thought about what he said. One November night I said good-night and put on my coat to go to my space, but it was cold and damp and windy. So I hung up my coat and went upstairs to my office. I stood in the middle of the floor and recalled Mike's words. I got a heavy wool blanket from the closet in my bedroom and spread it out on the floor. I put a candle in the middle of the blanket, lit it, turned off the light, got ready for bed and sat on the blanket with the candle and a bible.

It felt strange and I wanted to be outside. But I sat

cross-legged on the blanket for an hour. I did the same the following night and intermittently all during the winter when it was rainy or cold or too unpleasant to go outside. Some nights when it was nice outside I still came in after my walk, and sat for a while on the blanket. By early spring, the edges of the blanket marked the boundaries of my space.

One night the following spring I had sat on the blanket longer than usual. I became restless. Without adverting to anything particular except the fact that it was one o'clock in the morning and everyone had long since gone to bed, I stood up, blew out the candle and put it in its place on the shelf, put the bible on my desk and wrapped the heavy blanket around me. I opened the door of my room and padded barefoot down the stairs and out the back door. I walked out to the orchard, and as I walked a chant was running through my mind without my even hearing it: "I'm looking for a sacred place. I'm looking for a sacred place. I'm looking for a sacred place." I had walked for quite a distance, my pace keeping time with the chant in my mind, when I suddenly heard my chant. I said out loud, "I'm looking for a sacred place!" And I was surprised.

Aware now of what I was thinking and feeling, I headed for the far edge of the orchard. I sat down near one of the ancient apple trees and hoped to be found by God, but I was restless again in a very short time. I got up and walked toward the woods. I was halfway across the clearing between the orchard and the woods when out of the woods a figure moved toward me. I was stunned and afraid and embarrassed! Who could be up at this hour? I asked myself. What is he going to think when he sees me out here with only a blanket wrapped around me? I stood very still in the dark as the figure moved toward me. It was Mike! "What are you doing out here?" he asked me before I could ask him the same question.

Without considering what I would say, I blurted out, "I'm looking for a sacred place." He asked simply if he could join me. I said sure, and we walked. We began a conversation about something Mike had on his mind and finally returned to the house much later. I went right to bed.

The next morning I woke realizing that I had made a symbol. I had gone in search of being found by God. I had not found a sacred *place,* but I had made *space.* A particular place was not the point; the *journey* in search of a place to be found by God was what was important. The journey was a symbol. I had made a prayer with my feet.

The following night I again went on a journey, knowing now that my seeking for a place had provided the space. I had heard him knocking and had opened the door without realizing what I was doing.

On this second night I made the identical journey I had made the night before, but the journey was my space and my symbol. I stopped and stood under a pine tree on the edge of the clearing. As I stood there, a figure again emerged from the woods and walked across the clearing. It was Mike.

He came and stood beside me under the pine tree and was silent. Eventually I tilted my head back—way back—and peered up into the branches of the pine. "Maybe up there is a sacred place," I said. Mike didn't respond. Then I added quickly, "No, I don't think so; I'm afraid of heights." Mike remained silent. Then he said in the same simple way, "Don't you think you're going to have to climb it to find out?"

I told him maybe someday, but I doubted it.

The next night I walked by the tree and I knew I would have to climb it to find out. So I did. I didn't climb too far, about a quarter of the way up—maybe 10 or 12 feet from the ground. I found a comfortable, chairlike combination of branches and sat there for over an hour. And I heard him knocking.

I made many journeys after that, and found many sacred places—places where I was found by God. I climbed the pine tree often during that summer, and from those lower branches I could hear the cottonwood praying a short distance away. My journey took me to the chapel late at night, to my room, to the orchard and the woods, out past the grapevines. And I began to wonder if other people had sacred places. I started to ask them.

One young woman, 23 years old, said she went to the river outside town. She sat on a rock next to the river. "The flowing of the river reminds me of my God," she said. "Sometimes the river is swollen and its power and movement are obvious. In the winter when it is frozen, I still know it is flowing underneath. And that's the way I want God to be in my life—like a river force, always flowing, always giving direction."

Another young, recently married woman said she had no special place outside or anything like that. But as she ironed or did dishes, she would get the urge to pray. "So I don't do anything special. I just go into the living room and sit down and say the rosary, or just pray."

A young man told me he walked a half a mile or so outside town and climbed a steep hill and sat in the ruins of an old house. "I just go there and sit," he said. "And I expect to hear God and to discover him anew."

Another college-age man went into the woods and just sat by a stream, or he walked near his home, depending on his mood or the weather or the season of the year or the time of day. He, too, said that the journey was the important thing.

A 50-year-old mother of seven said she got up early in the morning and just sat in the breakfast nook "all alone and quiet before Jim and the kids are up."

A religious sister went into a field and just sat there. "I come here to get in touch with my own inner space," she said. "This place is sacred for me. And for me as a woman it has special meaning. I read somewhere, and I believe it is true in my own experience, that a woman reaches fulfillment when she decides whom or what she will admit to her inner space for keeps. I come here hoping to admit Jesus Christ to my inner space. And he finds me here."

Like me, all of them looked for a place in order to make space. And they all heard him knocking. The particular place was not the important item; making space was what they were doing. Part of that making space was being alone and being quiet for a long enough time.

In the fall of that year I was transferred from that rural setting in Indiana. I knew it was time to leave. I had been there for seven years. In late July some men cut down the cottonwood tree. It had often been struck by lightning, and they feared that if lightning struck it just one more time it might fall over and crush the garage which stood near it. Another man came in and trimmed all the trees on the property. He cut off all the lower branches of the pine tree so I couldn't climb it anymore.

The night before I left, I walked outside and stood in the clearing. I think I cried. No cottonwood murmuring its prayer, no way to climb the pine tree. No figure coming from the woods. The place was sacred; I knew that. God had found me there.

But the place had changed, and I was leaving. He would still knock. I would only have to make space—in a new place—and I would hear him.

I moved to an inner-city parish in a metropolitan area. I was not assigned to work in the parish, but I had an office there. I had to find new ways of making space. I went to a park in the city, especially a park near the lake. I went to the church. I sat in my room. I even found him knocking in a large shopping mall and in an airport.

I brought my blanket with me, and Mike's words continue to be a challenge: "I'm sure a man of your intelligence has found an alternative."

Finding the right place, the right time, and just being there alone long enough is the beginning of praying for me. And so I suggest that if you want to pray, make space.

2. Calming the Storm —Space Within

The beach was crowded; the day was hot. James leaned against the stern of one of the boats which had been pulled ashore, his feet in the water. Some kids (little kids, that is, . . . James was only a teenager himself) played in the sand and puddled around on the water's edge. The adults just sat and listened to the man who spoke to them from the boat just offshore. Peter and Andrew and John stood in the water beside the boat and held it from drifting as it rose and sank gently in the tide. Philip and a couple of the others were behind Jesus in the boat. Matthew sat in the boat on the shore against which James was leaning. All 12 of them were right there, only the fishermen among them feeling completely at home.

James listened as Jesus spoke. Everyone listened. But Jesus had selected James to be with him, so James listened a little more intently than the rest, he thought. There was a riddle here, and James figured he was supposed to grasp some special meaning in what Jesus said.

Jesus spoke about seeds and soil, about a seed grow-ing all by itself silently and about a mustard seed. It all had to do with something about the reign of God, but it wasn't clear. James knew he would have to think about it later and longer.

Jesus finished speaking and looked at James with a nod. James sprang from beside the beached fishing boat and leaped into the one Jesus sat in. Peter and Andrew and John swung out of the water and over the side of the boat. The rest came from the shore quickly. Only Mat-thew hesitated before getting his sandals wet. But he was pulled aboard as the boat pushed off.

"Let us cross over to the other shore," Jesus said to them. Leaving the crowd behind, they took him away in the boat in which he had been sitting. Jesus was tired and almost immediately he fell asleep on the cushion in the back of the boat.

James pondered what Jesus had said as Peter and Andrew pulled at the oars. Even when he took Andrew's place, James' mind was not on his rowing.

He hardly noticed the wind come up as the sun sank behind the shore they had just left. But the first wave which splashed against his leg brought him back to the task at hand. The sky darkened.

The others sat low in the boat and bailed water as fast as they could. The boat rose on one wave after another and crashed down again. More water, then rain, the hard-driving wind. They were supposed to be getting away from the hassle of the crowd and the busy day. So who needed a storm? Matthew was seasick. James couldn't remember ever before seeing Matthew in a boat. All he did was collect taxes on other people's boats! And even at that, the fishermen had to go to Matthew to pay the tax; he never came to them.

And Jesus was asleep. He had done a lot of talking, James thought to himself, but for what good? They were all going to drown. This was not the peaceful chance to reflect on his words after a day in the hot sun which James had planned on. And he was asleep! Could you believe it? He was asleep!

Finally James couldn't take it any longer. "Doesn't it matter to you that we're all going to drown?" he shouted over the roar of the wind and the waves. He reached for the pillow and yanked it from under Jesus' head. Jesus woke and rebuked the wind and then he said to the sea, "Quiet! Be still!" The wind fell off and everything grew calm. Then he looked at them all—but James thought he looked right at him only—and he said to them, "Why are you so terrified? Why are you lacking in faith?" A great awe came over them all. James heard Andrew say to Peter, "Who can this be that even the wind and the sea obey him?" But James just sat there for a minute, then climbed over the bench on which he had been sitting and let some-one else take the oar. He sat in the bottom of the boat next to Matthew. Matthew was useless and ill. James didn't feel much better, and he didn't even notice the water in which he sat.

I can't count the number of days and nights that I've gone to my space outside of myself in order to try to hear him knocking, only to find a storm brewing within me so violent that I might as well have been in a discotheque. There was no noise beating against my eardrums from the outside, but there was a din within. The orchard and woods were quiet enough, but I was worried about someone or something that had happened during the day. Or I was planning a workshop and my mind just wouldn't put it down. Or I was faced with a decision I didn't know how to make. Or I had yelled at someone during the day and now I felt foolish about it.

I have sat in my office and felt the urge—even the necessity—to pray because I felt I was called to it. And I've left my desk and sat down on the blanket, or I've gone to the church or outside. I've really wanted to reflect—

and reflect deeply—on what I had learned or read or
thought about. I've wanted to let some word from scripture sink more deeply into me. I've told myself I should
do it! But there was no way I could calm the storm within.

I have walked corridors of colleges in which I was
attending some workshop, sat in motel room chairs, walked
along the shore of Lake Michigan, driven through city
streets or just lain in bed and wanted to make the space
to hear him knocking. But as soon as I got away from
the hassle of the crowd or the pressures of the day, a storm
would come up. I pushed off for the calm of the other
shore, all right; but it seemed as if I never got there!

Many people I know find deep and satisfying meaning in thinking of prayer as making space in order to hear
him knocking. But after lots of attempts at it—and after
achieving some outer space—they become discouraged by
the crowding of their space within. "How do I get my mind
to be still?" they've asked me. I usually come up with some
sage advice, never adverting to the fact that I often can't
follow the advice I give them.

My own difficulty through many years has been that
I always compared every attempt to make space to those
times when it was easy to do so and there was no storm.
Sometimes simply making space outside myself was enough
to establish space within. But there have been—and there
are—other times. I've come to believe that those other
times are as normal as the quiet times. Praying means dealing with stormy times as well as with peaceful times.

The Gospels don't really mention James in the incident of the storm on the Sea of Galilee. I've just imagined
that. But by imagining the scene through his eyes, I've
learned something about myself and about dealing with
the storms within.

I've learned that making space within is not always a
matter of establishing a quiet vacuum or void or vacant
mind. It's not always a matter of simply clearing my mind
and heart of thoughts and concerns. Sometimes I can't

reflect peacefully on a word from scripture; I can't have it take root and grow, to crowd out other concerns. Sometimes I have to cry out, "Doesn't it matter to you that I'm going to drown? Doesn't it matter to you that I'm so preoccupied and distracted that I can't even think of you?"

Of course it matters to him; he's the one who is knocking. I'm the one who's distraught. I'm the one who's angry with myself because I'm so distraught. He simply continues to knock. When I realize his gentle, patient persistence, I can be more gentle with myself.

I often imagine that my mind is like a dog on a leash. I'm taking it for a walk. It wants to investigate every corner and object it passes. It doesn't want to walk calmly along my chosen path. I'm tempted to yank on the leash and make it follow more closely the path I want to walk. But I seem no sooner to get it back than it wanders off again.

I've learned TO BE A BIT MORE GENTLE. I try to coax it back now, gently tugging on the leash instead of yanking on it. Pulling and yanking only tire me out and make me angry and discouraged. It doesn't prevent wandering; it just makes me distraught.

One reason I try to get down to business when I go to pray is that I haven't planned to make enough space. I've got too little time to "get it in." I can't be wasting precious moments when I'm at prayer. And that simply means I've not provided enough outer space. I may be alone and even quiet; but I haven't enough time. I don't have time to wait and to waste. So I've learned TO TAKE MORE TIME when there is a storm within.

And I've learned TO CRY OUT TO THE LORD who seems to be unconcerned in the midst of my storm. And I've recognized an amazing thing in that cry. I've discovered, at a depth of me that was not touched by the storm, a hunger and a longing for God which is always there, beneath my preoccupations and distractions. Strangely, it seems that the surfacing of this agonized hunger is

almost always followed by a powerful word from the Lord
directed at my surface storm. "Quiet! Be still!"

One of my happiest moments in the past few years was
while I was giving a retreat to a group of college seminarians in Denver. They had asked for a retreat on prayer.
They wanted me to talk to them about prayer, and they
wanted to pray. After I had spoken to them in a few con-
ferences about the Lord knocking, and about making space
and making symbols, some were saying that nothing was
happening. They said they just could not pray. As they
talked, one after another, I could feel their pain and their
disappointment. "Brothers," I said, "the hunger you feel
inside IS God. He is with you. You could not even want
to be found and touched by God if he were not already
touching and moving you to seek to be found by him."
Even in the dimly lighted room I could see tears in some of
their eyes. And the storm ceased. They had heard the
powerful word, "Quiet! Be still!" and their hearts were
calm.

James and I and those seminarians had left the
crowded shore to go to the peace of the other side. We all
had our plans to contemplate the word spoken by the Lord.
But what we expected contemplation to look like never
happened for any of us. Frantic, finally we cried out. And
in our cry we came to know that he was with us all the
time.

In calm moments and in stormy ones we try to make
space for precisely this reason: "All who are led by the
Spirit of God are sons of God. You did not receive a spirit
of slavery leading you back into [a life of] fear, but a spirit
of adoption through which we cry out, 'Abba!' (that is,
'Father!'). The Spirit himself GIVES WITNESS WITH
OUR SPIRIT in bearing witness that we ARE God's children. But the Spirit helps us in our weakness, for we do not
know how to pray as we ought. But the Spirit himself makes
intercession for us with groanings which cannot be expressed in speech. He who searches hearts knows what the

Spirit means, for the Spirit intercedes for the saints as God himself wills" (Rom 8: 14-16; 26-27).

Every minute of every day, in calm and in storm, the Spirit of God who has been given to us is praying. If anyone attempts to make space enough for that prayer of the Spirit to break into consciousness, that person can deliberately and freely make the prayer of the Spirit his or her own. And what is the Spirit of God praying within us? Love, joy, peace, patience, kindness, goodness, trustfulness, consideration for others (gentleness), and self-control (Gal 5:22).

Those prayers are always there—just as radio and television waves are always in the atmosphere around us. I make space so they can erupt into consciousness—so I can tune in what the Spirit is praying. Sometimes I make that space in calm; at other times, in storm.

If there is any trick to making the space I need, it might be this: don't regard praying as one more necessary item on the agenda of the day's activities. Making space means that I allow time when nothing is scheduled. The mere fact that I wedge praying into a busy schedule may be for some enough to prevent space from happening.

Often I have wanted to find a discarded English dictionary and cut out all the words between "play" and "pray," between "reflect" and "relax." The two ideas are so closely related that something should be done to show their relationship. Praying is not a task I undertake in the same way I dig into all the other activities of my life. Praying is what I do during those moments or hours that I have freed from concerns and cares about accomplishing things; it is my chance to relax with the Lord simply because it is good to do so.

If you would pray, make space.

3. Stewing, Reflecting, Praying

The Christian tradition of praying had pretty shaky beginnings, and I've been faithful to that tradition in most of my praying. It's rare that I go to prayer from a calm, placid day. Yet somehow the image I've walked around with—the image of what the good prayerful life should look like—is this: from serene involvement in the peaceful enterprises of life—gardening, reading, speaking softly with others—I enter into some sacred place and raise my mind to God.

I don't ever remember such a day! I don't like gardening; I'm a poor reader; I usually talk loud. I'm usually too busy with things far removed from the natural and the humane. My life is filled with telephones, machines that don't work right, deadlines which have just passed without the job being finished, people who want to talk, cars that are a thousand miles past due for a tune-up, airplanes to catch or which haven't arrived on time, conventions to attend, interviews to conduct, talks or papers to be written, people to visit. Making space in the midst of all that is a trick. Space doesn't happen.

It has taken all the discipline I can muster to provide myself with an hour each day for being alone and being quiet and, even then, having space outside is no guarantee that there will be space within.   My mental machinery keeps churning.

This used to disturb me quite a bit. After all, I wanted to pray. I would go to prayer and fight off distractions until I wearied of the effort. I'd find brief intervals amid the distractions during which I'd advise God on how best to run our world, or at least my life. It seemed that when I wanted to pray, all I did was stew about life.

I still do the same thing; but now I allow myself to do so without trying to interrupt or cut short the stewing. I let it come; I get it all out; and only then will I be satisfied and still enough to hear what he might have to say.

This way of praying started the very day Jesus was raised to new life. Two of his disciples were getting out of town after it was all over. They were walking to a place about seven miles from Jerusalem. As they walked along they were rehashing all that had been going on in Jerusalem the last few days.

As they really got into rehearsing the events of the past few days and the meaning those events had for them personally, Jesus began to walk with them, but they didn't recognize that it was Jesus.

"What are you discussing as you go your way?" he asked them. Well, what *would* they be discussing, Cleopus said to himself; there was only one thing to discuss. He was upset at the events, and even more upset that someone should not know about those events.

"Are you the only one in town who doesn't know what's been going on there these past few days?"

"What things?" Jesus asked.

Well, that was a little much! It didn't seem possible that anyone could have missed out on all the excitement. So Cleopus started out the narration: he told the whole story of the tragedy he and his friends had experienced. He told this ill-informed and unperceptive stranger all about Jesus—how he was a good man, but he was killed. He told of the hope he and his friends had entertained: "We were hoping he was the one who would set Israel free." He told of the women going to the tomb and finding it empty, and about some others going to the tomb to verify the women's story. Sure enough, it was just as they had said; but they saw nothing of him—that was the worst part!

Then Jesus said to them, "What little faith you have! How slow you are to believe the *whole* message of the prophets. Didn't the Messiah have to suffer all these things and so enter into his glory?" Then he started back at the beginning, with Moses and the prophets, and helped them see that maybe things had gone exactly as they were supposed to have gone.

By now they had reached the village they had set out for. He said good-bye to them as they started to look for a room in which to spend the night. But they pressed him to stay with them. "It's almost evening—the day is almost done." So he went in with them.

While they were sharing their meal of bread and wine, he blessed and broke the bread, and only then did they catch on. It was Jesus! But he had disappeared from their sight. They looked at each other and said, "Weren't our hearts burning up inside of us as he talked to us on the road and explained the scriptures to us?" They got up and headed right back to Jerusalem. They found the rest of the company and were told that the women's story was true; Jesus was alive. They said, "Yes, we know. He walked with us on the road to Emmaus."

The two disciples made space outside themselves, all right; they had about a two-hour walk ahead of them. But their space within was cluttered with their own experience of life, their sadness, their depression. Their space inside was so cluttered that they didn't recognize Jesus when he came and walked with them. Yet Jesus didn't make any attempt to draw them away from their concerns. He even asked them what they were talking about.

They gave him a brief, general statement of their concern: "Those things which have caused all the excitement in town." But Jesus invited them to go even more deeply into their stewing over those events: "What things?" he asked them. So they launched off on the telling of the story of Jesus—the events of the drama and their own hopes and disappointments. Even some subsequent details.

Stewing about the events and the preoccupations of life is a good way to begin prayer. I feel invited to do that by the Lord himself. "What things?" he asks. So I tell him. I tell him about the events and about my reactions to those events—the hope and the disappointment, the success and the failure, the triumph and the defeat, the joy and the sorrow—the whole thing in every detail. It's important only that I tell it *to him*—not simply to myself. I stew in his presence. I listen to myself stew.

But we shouldn't stop there. Run to the end of your story; tell it again. Fill in details, but run to the point where you become silent, because you've said it all. He did, after all, ask "What things?"

Then step back from your stewing. Imagine a film director calling for the camera to pull back from the scene. You've been sitting right on the edge of the scene to do your stewing over your concerns. Your attention has been on the scene in front of you. Now that you pull away, you can see yourself sitting there. Reflect on yourself sitting there, poring over the scene. Reflect on your stewing. What position have you taken to do your stewing? How are you looking at the things which concern you?

The disciples on their way out of town told their sad story, and then stepped back enough to see that the position they had assumed in relation to the events they narrated was this: they had a plan for salvation; they knew what the messiah should look like, and those plans were frustrated. They thought the events precluded salvation, but it was their perspective on those events which prevented them from seeing the mystery of salvation unfold.

I believe that if we will cry or shout or pout or giggle out the whole story, and then reflect on the position we have assumed in relation to the story, we might hear him say, "How foolish you are! How slow to believe!" I have often advised God on how he should have done something in order to bring about my or someone else's salvation. I've told him what the events should have looked like. And then he gently tells me that there's nothing wrong with the events; the problem is with my perspective or attitude toward those events.

Like the two of them on the dusty road on a Sunday morning, I've told God of my plan for the salvation and welfare of myself and my friends. It's only when I finish stewing and pause to reflect on my perspective that I can come to know that I'm not God, but I've pretended to be; that I'm not all-loving, but I've pretended to be. It's only after I've finished stewing and stepped back to reflect on myself stewing that there's any chance for me to hear him say, "How foolish you are! How slow to believe the *whole* message of the prophets!"

Jesus went back into the religious and spiritual tradition which had formed the two disciples. He invited them to view the events of the past few days from the perspective of that religious tradition. He asked them to rummage around in their own tradition to see if it might not be advanced by viewing it in the light of the events of the past few days. He invited them to look to see if their tradition didn't shed light on those events. They responded to the invitation. "Weren't our hearts burning up inside us as he talked to us on the road and explained the scriptures to us?"

That's the process of reflecting all of us are called to do if we are to enter seriously into prayer: to look at the positions we have taken and from which we view life. Many of us feel that our life is a matter of producing and directing a film for God's viewing. We believe in our hearts that

we know what we and others should do in order to establish
his kingdom on earth. And when we or others fail to move
in the scene according to the script we have written or con-
ceived, we want to say, "Cut!" We want to run it through
again.

But if we can learn to get done with our stewing and
reflect on our attitudes and positions, we may eventually
be led to see that our role in establishing the kingdom of
God is to allow him to have his way with us. We are not
the producer/director; we are the product. To be sure, we
have a role to play, but our role is not to determine the
outcome of the scene. God can use success *and* failure,
joy *and* sorrow, victory *and* defeat to bring to completion
the work he has begun in us.

In my own vocabulary I have reserved the word
"prayer" for a very special segment of the process of
making ourselves available to God. I know that the whole
arena of making space and making symbols, the entire
endeavor of stewing, reflection, praying, can rightly be
called prayer. But after the disciples on the road to Emmaus had made space outside (their two hours on the
road) and had made their interior space (listened to Jesus
speak to them, stewed over the events of their lives, reflected on their viewpoint) they got to the very core of
praying. They turned their *attention to Jesus directly*—
no longer to things about him or reflection on their own
perspective. Turning their attention to him, they *reached
out to him from their hearts.* "Stay with us," they pressed
him.

It was then that they experienced intimacy with him
and recognized, not only his presence then and there at
the table, but also his presence to them throughout the day,
and his presence in the events which had concerned them.

After we have stewed and reflected, we can turn our
face and our heart to God and speak whatever our heart of
hearts suggests. It is only after we have stewed and spoken
all those words that we can speak personally from our

hearts directly to the Lord. It is often only after we have reflected and, through a return to our theological and spiritual tradition, have heard a word from the Lord about our activity that we can hear his word spoken personally and directly to us.

Stewing, reflecting, praying are not so much steps to be followed one after the other; they are phases in our praying which can be recognized. The reason it is important to recognize these phases is so we avoid breaking off our praying before we have reached the core. Often we quit after we have stewed. Perhaps when we reflect we catch ourselves in some attitude or outlook which we know is not completely in line with what we know we should be, and then we quit.

But prayer becomes most beneficial for us when we stay at it until we are face-to-face with the living God and are speaking to him from our heart of hearts and are hearing him in the depths of our spirits. We should remain with those sentiments of our hearts as long as we can, without trying overmuch to prolong them.

I have often felt that, given an hour for prayer, I would stew for 58 minutes, reflect for 90 seconds, and pray for 30 seconds. That is something of an exaggeration, but I know this: it often takes a lot of time for me to come to the end of my stewing before I can glimpse my own spiritual position. And only then can I turn to God and hear him clearly and speak to him plainly.

At other times, stewing takes very little time; reflecting takes more time; praying seems to flow very easily and very early. It all depends on something over which I have very little control. I'm sure that the disciples on the road to Emmaus weren't concerned about making a good prayer. That first day of the new age of the Resurrection found them concerned with the life they lived and the events they experienced. It was in stewing, reflecting and praying that they eventually found the Lord in their lives and experienced his presence to them. The Christian tradition of praying had pretty shaky beginnings. We can rely on those beginnings to give us some indication of how we should pray in our own era.

Precisely how stewing and reflecting and praying are done, or how each individual gets the most out of those activities, aren't of great importance. It does seem important, though, to allow ourselves to experience these rather spontaneous activities and to gain from them the sense of prayer they give. It's not so much the particular events of a day which determine whether or not prayer is possible; it's much more a matter of how those events are dealt with.

If prayer can be found in the events discussed on the Emmaus road, it can be found in a day filled with phones, planes, deadlines, conventions, talks, and interviews.

If you want to pray, make space.

4. The Urge to Make Symbols

Almost everything I've ever read about prayer seems to suggest that it is a pleasant, logical, satisfying experience which makes sense. This is not always—or even usually—my experience of prayer. I'd have to admit, and am glad to say, that praying regularly has made my life make a lot more sense. But the ways I've tried to make myself available to God have not always been satisfying; the expectations with which I've gone to prayer have not always been realized; the results of my praying have sometimes been unpleasant. As often as not, not my methods, nor my expectations, nor the results of my praying have made much sense.

I have lived most of my life with an idealized notion of what relating to God should look like. This caused me to look for the interior and exterior space in which I hoped to hear him knocking. But for a long time I identified my external space so rigidly with some specific place, and my internal space with some particular sentiments, that I sometimes felt that I could not pray because I was in the wrong place or in the wrong mood. Even if I was in my favorite place to pray, and had managed to quiet the storm within, I often didn't open the door when I heard him knocking because I thought that the way I was couldn't be acceptable to him. I tried always to choose ways of expressing myself which I judged to be "proper" expressions. Sometimes the problem was that I knew myself not to be as "proper" as the prayer form with which I tried to express myself. At other times the symbols I had learned served very well to express how I was.

I have come to think of the whole process of praying as an attempt to make myself available to God in order to be touched and moved by him. It is making a series of symbolic openings by which I allow God to enter my life. I have begun to believe that all Christian life is walking the path Jesus walked—not in the details of his earthly life, but in the movement of the mystery of his life—the Paschal Mystery.

One of the most familiar expressions of the Paschal Mystery is the hymn in Paul's letter to the Philippians. This hymn has shaped my perception of the whole Christian life. As beautiful and lofty as it is, it is also practical. Everything Paul wrote was for a practical purpose—to lead his Christian converts closer to their God. I think we do Paul an injustice and ourselves a disservice when we read too piously what he wrote so powerfully.

This is a theological hymn about Jesus, and it is the heart of Paul's exhortations on living practical Christian lives. He says:

> Have in yourselves the same mind that was in Christ:
>   Though he was in the form of God,
>   he did not deem equality with God
>   something to be grasped at.
>   Rather, he emptied himself
>   and took the form of a slave,
>   being born in human likeness.

> He was known to be of human estate,
>   and it was thus that he humbled himself,
>   obediently accepting even death,
>   death on the cross!
> Because of this
>   God highly exalted him
>   and bestowed on him the name
>   above every other name,
> So that at Jesus' name
>   every knee must bend
>   in the heavens, on the earth
>   and under the earth,
>   and every tongue proclaim
>   to the glory of God the Father:
>   Jesus Christ is Lord!

In this hymn Paul expresses the three movements of the Mystery of Jesus: a downward movement from equality with God to our human condition; a movement farther downward to the acceptance even of death; the upward movement of resurrection into newness of life.

These are the movements of the Paschal Mystery as Jesus lived and experienced them, and they have ever since been the norm of all Christian life. "Have in you the same mind that was in Christ!" Salvation for us Christians consists in our participation in the three movements of the Mystery of Jesus: not to cling to equality with God but to become what all people are; to accept even death; to be raised to newness of life. Sin is the refusal to enter this mystery at one of its levels: to cling to equality with God and refuse to accept the human condition; to refuse and flee from death; to refuse to accept and acknowledge the newness of life which is ours.

What are the meaning and ramifications of the experience of Jesus' emptying of himself? It means that he actually took on our human condition; he became everything that we are. The entire human experience was his.

Since that event, *nothing truly human* can ever again separate us from God. God and humanity are united in a way which rules out forever any justification to the claim that we cannot be united to God because of some human quality of ours. Our bodies don't separate us from God; our moods don't; our experiences of joy, fun, grief, anger, emotions of every kind—these can't separate us from God. Our sexuality can't. Suffering can't. Even temptation cannot separate us from God. The only thing which can separate us from God is our free choice to be less than human or to be more than human—to cling to equality with God.

Jesus' acceptance of death has meaning and ramifications for our lives. To grasp that meaning, we may have to lay aside some of our own ideas about the meaning of death and listen intently to what the gospel writers say.

We tend to think of death medically: the cessation of the pulmonary functions or the discontinuance of brain waves. Or we think of death as a religious event: the separation of body and soul. But the gospel writers present the death of Jesus as his victory, his glorification. They present the death of Jesus as his shedding of human limitations while still remaining human. In his earthly life he was bound by the limitations of time and place, but in death he shed those limitations so he could be present to all time and to every place. He could not give the Spirit, Saint John tells us, because he had not yet been glorified. But in his dying he handed over the Spirit. From his body broken in death, the Spirit filled the whole world as from the broken jar the fragrance of the ointment filled the whole house.

"We who have been baptized into Christ have been baptized into his death," Paul says. Our baptism is a commitment to shed our human limitations of sin and selfishness.

The third movement of the Paschal Mystery is, perhaps, the most profound of all. In being raised to newness of life, Jesus continues to be God's revelation of his great plan of salvation.

One of my teachers used to say, "The Resurrection isn't meant to prove something to nonbelievers; it is meant to reveal something to those who are willing to believe." The New Testament gives no account of Jesus' actual rising from the dead. No one saw him rise, scenes depicted in church windows notwithstanding.

If the Resurrection was meant to prove something, we'd have to admit it was rather poorly handled! Jesus didn't appear to his enemies. (Imagine Pilate's amazement if Jesus had stood at his breakfast table on that Sunday morning!) He didn't even appear to crowds in Jerusalem. He appeared only to those who were willing to believe. And he did so to reveal something to them.

First, his appearance revealed that he is alive! This same Jesus who was dead is now alive.

Second, his appearance revealed that he is alive in a new and mysterious way. There is always something eerie about him: his friends don't recognize him right away, and when they do, the old familiarity is gone. He hasn't come back to life; he has been raised to newness of life!

Third, he is alive in a new and mysterious way in which he no longer comes and goes, he's simply present! If you read the accounts of his life before the Resurrection, you will see that we are told how Jesus came and went: "He got into a boat and crossed over to the other side." "As he made his way along the Sea of Galilee. . . ." "He came back to Capernaum." "Another time, while he went walking along the lakeshore. . . ."

But after the Resurrection there is no mention of how he comes or goes. In English the structure of those sentences is awkward, but the literal translation of the original Greek would be: "Morning came and Jesus stood on the shore." "Mary turned around and there stood Jesus." "The doors were locked and Jesus stood in their midst." Only in the record of the journey to Emmaus are we told how he goes: "He disappeared from their sight."

All these accounts are records of how Jesus revealed

to his disciples that he was present to them. There is no
human event to which he is not present now. St. John
expressed this in the Book of Revelation in chapters four
and five:

> After this I had another vision: above me
> there was an open door to heaven, and I heard
> the trumpet-like voice which had spoken to me
> before. It said, "Come up here and I will show
> you what must take place in time to come. . . ."
> In the right hand of the One who sat on the
> throne I saw a scroll. It had writing on both
> sides and was sealed with seven seals. Then I saw
> a mighty angel who proclaimed in a loud voice:
> "Who is worthy to open the scroll and break its
> seals?" But no one in heaven or on earth or under
> the earth could be found to open the scroll or
> examine its contents. I wept bitterly because no
> one could be found worthy to open the scroll and
> examine it.
> One of the elders said to me: "Do not weep.
> The Lion of the Tribe of Judah, the Root of
> David, has won the right by his victory to open
> the scroll with the seven seals."
> Then, between the throne with the four
> living creatures and the elders, I saw a Lamb
> standing, a Lamb that had been slain. . . . The
> Lamb came and received the scroll from the right
> hand of the One who sat on the throne. When
> he had taken the scroll, the four living creatures
> and the twenty-four elders fell down before the
> Lamb. . . . This is the new hymn they sang:

> > Worthy are you to receive the scroll
> >   and break open its seals,
> >   for you were slain.
> > With your blood you purchased for God
> >   men of every race and tongue,
> >   of every people and nation.

> You made of them a kingdom
> and priests to serve our God,
> and they shall reign on the earth.

In this passage John is expressing a theology of resurrection and its implications for us. John is invited in his vision to "come up here and I will show you what must happen hereafter." In the scroll are written all the events of human history, and no one can open that scroll and be present to all those events except the Lamb who is standing—alive, but with the marks of slaughter on him. Only the risen Lord, alive with a new and mysterious life in which he no longer comes and goes but is simply present, can be present to every event of human history.

The believers' first expression of their faith in the risen Lord was simply to confess: "Jesus is Lord!" He had been given that name which is above every name—the name that was reserved for God—"Lord." Their confession meant that they believed that Jesus is present to and has dominion over every human event.

This third movement of the Paschal Mystery has ramifications for the believer. We are to believe that every human experience has been raised to a new level: Jesus is Lord of every human event. We and all our life experiences are raised to newness of life. No matter what we experience, we can proclaim that Jesus is alive and present and has dominion over those experiences, and that through those very experiences of our lives he can bring to completion in us the work he has begun.

In Chapter four of his letter to the Philippians Paul says: "Rejoice in the Lord always! I say it again: Rejoice! Let your imperturbability be evident to all; the Lord is very near." The word which I have translated as "imperturbability" is translated in many ways. Basically it means the state of mind and spirit which the Stoics sought for—tranquility brought about by having no selfish concerns for one's self.

Even though Paul uses the Stoics' word, he gives a
very different reason for rejoicing: Christians can remain
unperturbed by life's events, because the Lord is very near.
The Lord is present to and has dominion over every event
of life; because he is Lord of everything that Christians
experience, the believer can have confidence that, whether
those events are pleasant or not, they will work out for his
good. Through those events God brings to completion
the work he has begun.

Jesus experienced three movements of the Paschal
Mystery: becoming what all people are—truly human;
accepting death and thereby shedding human limitations;
being raised to newness of life and thus becoming present
to every event of human history. Our new life comes as we
are inserted more and more fully into this Paschal Mystery
by ceasing to pretend we are God and accepting our human
condition, by shedding our human limitations of sin and
selfishness, and by living each event of our lives in openness—allowing Jesus' dominion over the events of our
lives to bring to completion the work he has begun in us.

This process in us is not a once-in-a-lifetime occur-
rence. It happens over and over again. But it isn't just
going around the same circle time after time. It's more like a
spiral: each experience of more fully accepting our humanity, of shedding sin and selfishness, of confessing that Jesus
is Lord of the events of our life—each experience of this
mystery brings us closer to holiness, until we can say, with
Paul, "It is now no longer I who live, but Christ lives
in me."

At each stage of life, and during each day of our lives,
we can again experience the cycle of being "known to be of
human estate," of "accepting even death" and of being
"raised high." We may experience plateaus when the
radical significance of the Paschal Mystery is not felt, but
it will again and again become a crucial challenge to us
and invite us to "have in you the mind which was in Christ
Jesus."

Praying is making space and making symbols which open us to God to be touched and moved by him. The mystery that God is working out in us is the Paschal Mystery of his Son. We can expect that the point of all our praying will be to recognize and accept our human condition, to accept even the death of shedding sin and selfishness, and to be raised to newness of life. The symbols we use for our praying should be expressive of our conscious and free openness to having the mystery of Christ played out more fully in us.

Sometimes we select from the symbols we have learned: as for example when we use the words of prayers formulated by generations of believing, praying people. Those words can be expressive of some aspect of our human condition of dependence or helplessness or repentance—eternally valid stances which human beings can always take before God. Or we can select traditional postures, practices or gestures: kneeling and standing, fasting, almsgiving, using raised or folded hands. Sometimes we select words and gestures which express our willingness to die to sin and selfishness. At other times we select symbols which express our belief that Jesus is Lord of the events of our lives, our submission to him and our joy at his dominion.

On the other hand, we don't have to select traditional or learned symbols for our praying; we can simply use symbolic words, gestures and practices of our own making. The more closely these homemade symbols reflect the great traditional symbols, the more likely they are to make us fully available—as we are—to the God who knocks and seeks admittance into our lives.

All this sounds quite theological and theoretical, but I didn't learn it that way. I have reflected on my own experience over the years and have only now arrived at this articulation. I remember some of the events of my life which helped me to realize that it was the Paschal Mystery I was experiencing. I want to invite you once again to the clearing between the orchard and the woods and share with you an evening which I remember as both joyful and embarrassing.

I believe I have a tendency to want to be God. I pretend to be secure and stable and bright and insightful. But often I feel very fragile. On several nights during my first years of living next to the orchard and the woods, I felt very weak and vulnerable. Several times the thought came to me to take off my clothes and stand naked under the sky. (I told you this would be embarrassing!) But I was too inhibited to entertain the impulse seriously. On more than one occasion I walked out to the clearing for the express purpose of standing naked under the heavens. But I couldn't do it.

One night I was very troubled and went out to walk and pray. As I did so, I lay on my back in the clearing and looked at the black sky above and the bright stars scattered in the heavens. As I lay there, I became angry at God for allowing things in my life to go as they had. My imagination conjured up the possibility of getting away from God.

As I lay there, the sky was framed by the trees on all sides. If I strained my eyes to look toward my toes, I could see the tops of the oak trees. I wondered if I could get up and run to the north far enough to get out from under the sky. But I concluded that I could run all the way to the neighboring town and would still be overmantled by the sky. Straining again, I cast my eyes upward toward the south. Could I run out into the countryside beyond the tips of those trees which bordered the southern edge of the clearing, and get out from under the sky? No, I couldn't. Neither north nor south, neither east nor west provided a way to escape the dominion of the sky above.

Then I wondered if I could make the sky go away, since I couldn't get away from it. I closed my eyes and stuck out my tongue. The sky didn't even wince. I squinted and wrinkled up my face into a contortion. When I opened my eyes the sky was still there. I stood up and twirled around and around until I was dizzy. Staggering, I looked up. Still the sky was there. I began to stamp my feet and flail with my arms and stick out my tongue! When I finally stopped, exhausted almost, I still saw the sky. It wouldn't go away. Throwing aside my sense of propriety, I did what I thought was outrageous: I pulled off my clothes and flung them as far as I could—deliberately, not in frenzy. I wanted to do something so outrageously rebellious that the sky would hide from me. I stood there naked and raised my eyes. Still the sky was looking peacefully down on me.

As I stood there, peace returned to my spirit. The sky became for me a symbol of God's faithfulness. I couldn't get away from him and I couldn't make him go away from me. In allowing myself to make symbols expressive of how I really was, I opened the door and admitted him.

He came in, and I experienced intimacy with him. First with my imagination, then with my actions I expressed symbolically just where I knew myself to be—angry at God and testing his faithfulness. I experienced my "human estate," I let go of my selfishness and I accepted that Jesus is Lord even of those events which I angrily rejected as having escaped God's dominion. I was asked and then helped to let go of the position I had assumed—a position in which I pretended to be God, with my own plan for how things should happen.

The urge to make symbols is in us, I'm convinced. We are drawn to make symbols expressive of how we actually are. And it is by doing so that we open the door to let him in. If I am too concerned with what proper prayer should look like, or if I suspect that something truly human can separate me from God, I'm liable to go through the motions of prayer without ever getting around to making myself available to God to be touched and moved by him.

If, however, I make the space to hear him knocking, and if I make symbols which open the door to admit him in to me as I know myself to be, then I make myself available to him to bring to completion in me the work he has begun—the Paschal Mystery of his Son.

I recently heard a group talking about a man in his 40s—a maintenance mechanic for a rather large building. He was a man of simple and direct faith, very active in his parish. He had been elected to the parish council and had worked very hard to help develop all aspects of the life of the parish. But he felt like he was weak in his faith. He often felt like a hypocrite in his parish activities because he knew himself internally to be as full of doubt as he outwardly appeared to be full of faith. But he continued to work, lacking the enthusiasm and inspiration he thought he should have.

The parish council decided on a day of recollection for themselves, and they went to a nearby retreat center for the day. The man hesitated to go; he even toyed with the idea of resigning from the parish council before they went for their day of prayer. How could he pray? he thought; he didn't even know if he believed anymore.

He went with the group to the retreat center. He was shown to his room. He stood there and said to himself, "What am I doing here?" He flopped down on the bed and sighed, "Jesus, I'm tired."

Today the man still tells the story of how he felt a great sense of peace come to him at that moment. Those who know him continue to tell of the new vitality with which he works for the good of the parish.

When I heard the story I couldn't help but think of the urge within us to make symbols. The man had been faithful to what he knew to be proper symbols of prayer. He benefitted from them, but they weren't able to do *everything* his spirit craved. When he finally allowed his spirit to seek its own expression of his human condition, he made himself available to God. Today he bears witness to anyone who asks that he was touched and moved by God. He opened the door, and God did come in.

Since I have started looking at life and at the attempts

of Christians to pray in this light, I've found a lot of simple life-events make a lot more sense. Taking the Paschal Mystery as the model of all Christian prayer has given me a way of seeing the things which I and others do, and that way of seeing things has enriched my life perhaps as much as has allowing myself to make my own kind of symbols.

Shortly after I heard the story of the man who was tired, I spoke with a priest about his experience of Lent. Shortly before Ash Wednesday he felt that maybe he should give up cigarettes for Lent. He gave voice to his urge in the presence of the other men in the rectory and, almost on a dare, all four of them decided to quit smoking until Easter. It was no more than that, but it prompted all of them to give up the smoking habit.

About halfway through Lent, the one who had initially felt the urge began taking time each day with scripture. He even began praying his breviary with much more faithfulness and regularity. He found that not smoking had become a kind of emptying which allowed room for something else, something better.

He realized with a great deal of satisfaction that he didn't need the cigarettes, which led him to look at what else in his life he might not need. He decided after three weeks that he didn't need television, which in turn gave him more time to read scripture and pray.

During the fourth week of Lent, he raised the question: "Do I need scripture? Would my life be different, would I feel a loss of direction in my life, if I didn't pray the scriptures daily?" And he concluded that his life would not be much different if he never opened the bible.

This didn't please him, but it led him to look very radically at his life. He saw that a lot of his life was determined by the habit he had developed of responding to his own and to other people's expectations. "I'm playing a game," he finally said; "sometimes other people's games. But it's always a game."

I don't know what this priest is doing these days. He

may have again taken up the habits of smoking, television
watching and playing his own and others' "priest-games."
But his urge to stop responding automatically to his own
"need" for a cigarette is a symbolic opening which allowed
God to enter his life more fully. He told me that for the
first time all the old-fashioned talk about Lent being a time
of emptying made sense to him. And to me the old-
fashioned word "mortification" (which means literally
"making death") made new sense. I believe his own spirit
led him to "accept even death" and to experience being
raised to newness of life.

I suppose I could think of a lot of other examples of
my own and other people's urge to make symbols, and find
in them lots of meaning for myself and for others. But this
is enough for my purposes here. We all have urges to make
symbols of our own, I believe. And that's good.

Often since my night in the clearing I've reflected on
my own very personal expression of myself in prayer and
its relationship to the expressions of prayer in my religious tradition. And I've wondered if a psalmist many
years prior to my night in the clearing didn't have a similar
experience. Whoever wrote Psalm 89 prayed:

> I will sing of your steadfast love, O Lord, forever;
>   with my mouth I will proclaim your faithfulness
>   to all generations.
> For your steadfast love was established forever,
>   your faithfulness is firm as the heavens. . . .
> Let the heavens praise your wonders, O Lord,
>   and your faithfulness.   (RSV)

The marvelous experience for me is this: in letting my
spirit have the freedom to find expression in prayer—by
making symbols which are intensely personal and very immediate, I got in touch with a human experience of openness to God which is shared by many others. I came to a
classic prayer form which has found expression in great
religious and spiritual literature.

Had I taken up the classic prayer form, but denied myself the personal expression, the odds are that the classic expression would always have remained for me something desirable but only partially mine. Now it is mine completely, and I know I share it with those who have prayed throughout the ages.

If you would pray, make symbols.

5. Homemade Symbols

I've already described some of the times when I felt urged to make my own symbols, but hesitated to allow myself to do so, and I've told of the good results for my own praying of having permitted myself to make my own kind of symbols. I share my experiences for this reason: when I simply generalize about the importance of symbols in praying, I find myself saying things which make prayer seem logical, pleasant, satisfying and always full of good sense. While prayer is all these things, I am convinced I've cheated myself when I've neglected those parts of me which are messy and not so nice.

I'd like to share some more thoughts and examples of making spontaneous symbols—some of my own and some which others have shared with me. I offer them not for imitation, but in the hope that they will encourage others to be more free in choosing or making the kind of symbols their own spirits suggest.

We don't make symbols with a hammer and saw; they are made by our creative religious imagination. With this imagination we can see and feel and sense meanings beyond the surface meaning of persons, events and things. We can see them anew, and in seeing them we make symbols.

I begin by telling you another story of my own wrestling with the urge to make symbols.

It was Holy Thursday. Nine months after I had moved to the city, I had returned to that friary in Indiana to give a series of talks to a group of young men who were thinking of entering religious life. I was to speak to them the following morning on the Paschal Mystery. I knew I was going to urge them to make space and make symbols.

While I was back in town, I decided to go for a physical to the local doctor who had been my doctor while I lived there. He is from India. After he finished examining me, he asked, "How long are your Good Friday services tomorrow?" I told him that they would probably last about an hour and a half.

He told me, "My wife and I are looking for the longest service we can find. In our tradition in India, the whole community gathers in the early morning and they fast all day. They pray and have services until about four o'clock in the afternoon, and break their fast with a simple meal which the whole community shares. Then they return to their homes."

As I walked home from the doctor's office, I thought over the profound symbols that community made in their attempt to celebrate Good Friday. My own liturgical tradition, which I love so much, seemed to be too limited in the time it took to celebrate the great event of the death of the Lord.

That evening, after we celebrated the Lord's supper with the friars and the people from town and the young men who were contemplating entering religious life, I sat down to put the final touches on the talk I was to give the young men the following morning—Good Friday. As I read over the end of the talk I was going to give, I began to feel a little bit hypocritical. I was going to urge the men to make the symbols they thought of, and to do so with abandon. I was going to urge them to let nothing—inconvenience, embarrassment, difficulty—nothing keep them from opening themselves to the Lord in the ways their spirits suggested. And as I read over the words I was going to speak, I knew there was one symbol I had wanted to make for years, but had not made. It seemed entirely too difficult and inconvenient, so I had found ways to avoid doing it.

I prayed that night before I went to bed, and I committed myself to make the symbol the following day—Good Friday. I determined to fast from solid food all during the day. Then in the evening I would do what my heart had suggested for several years. I had wanted to experience in some way other than in my mind the meaning of the words written in the Second Letter of Peter: "So we are even more confident of the message proclaimed by the prophets. You will do well to pay attention to it, because it is like a lamp shining in a dark place, until the Day dawns and the light of the Morning Star shines in your hearts."

Often I had thought of spending a whole night in vigil waiting for the dawn. Before I fell asleep on Holy Thursday night, I committed myself to fast all the next day from solid food and to spend the following night outside in the orchard with a candle, waiting for the dawn to appear.

Friday morning I gave my talk on the Paschal Mystery and urged the guys to make space and make symbols. All day I made plans for spending the evening and all night making the symbol I had resisted so long. While everyone was at supper, I walked to a nearby grocery store and bought one apple, one small piece of cheese, a French roll and a small bottle of wine. I put them in my room. I planned to spend the night until sunrise with the scriptures

and whatever kind of prayer would be possible or would
present itself. Then I'd break my fast at sunrise. Fruit,
cheese, bread and wine—they were all foods which were
symbolic to me of God's loving care. "The whole thing
may prove to be a flat nothing!" I wrote in my green book,
"or it might be a real prayerful night. I guess I don't really
care too much. I just want to do it."

I wandered around and talked with whomever I met
during the early evening of Good Friday, but my mind was
on making my symbol. About 11 o'clock I went to my
room and began to study scripture. The next morning I
was supposed to give a talk on the role of the Holy Spirit
in our lives. Following the advice of Peter's Second Letter
that I should keep my eyes fixed on the message of the
prophets, I began with the reading from Isaiah about the
suffering servant: "Here is my servant whom I uphold, my
chosen one with whom I am pleased, upon whom I have
put my Spirit." Then I followed the references given in
the footnotes to other passages from the the Old and New
Testaments about the Spirit of God.

About 2:00 a.m. I packed up my wine and bread and
cheese and apple and blanket. I tiptoed down the stairs
and got a candle stub out of the sacristy. Then I headed
for the far west edge of the apple orchard.

I chose a tree under which I had often prayed and set
the candle—about three inches tall—down in the grass. I
lighted it; the glow was embarrassingly bright. I sat down,
wrapped in the blanket, facing east, with the candle between me and that part of the horizon where the sun would
eventually appear.

I searched inside myself for a prayer that might be
there. But I was so distracted by the brightness of the light
from the candle that I couldn't pray. I moved the candle
farther away from me—now about six feet away. Again I
tried to find words with which to pray. But I couldn't find
any profound thoughts to put into words, so I simply com-
mended to the Lord whoever came to my mind.

I got very drowsy and almost fell asleep. So I got up and walked around the orchard. I could say only, "I'm tired! I'm hungry!" I walked some more and then came back to my spot near the candle. It was so clearly visible from a distance that I was afraid it would be seen by someone. But I couldn't imagine who'd be up!

At 4:00 a.m. I was looking at my watch and realizing that sunrise was still two hours away. (I had checked the local newspaper earlier that day for the exact time the sun would rise.) No matter how I tried to find some nice thoughts, the only thing that came to mind was that I was hungry and I was waiting for some sign of dawn in the eastern sky. I kept looking at the eastern horizon, then at the western—trying to see if there was any difference in their degrees of darkness. There wasn't.

I almost fell asleep a couple more times. So I alternately walked around the orchard or sat on the blanket. Some passages of Psalms began to come to mind, all of them about hunger and waiting for the dawn. "More than watchmen wait for the dawn, let Israel wait for the Lord." "Be stouthearted and wait for the Lord."

Gradually I began to walk around more widely and with more feeling of freedom. As I did so, I began a series of prayers in the ancient Jewish tradition. "Blessed are you, Lord, the God of all creation. You give us earth and sky and trees to walk upon and under and among. You give us the grace to recognize them as your gifts."

"Blessed are you, Lord, the God of all creation. You give us bodies which feel hunger and tiredness, and feet to walk about your creation. Let my walking and my tiredness and my hunger help me know of my need for you and of your presence to me."

There were other prayers like that, but I can't remember them now.

This went on for quite a while, and finally I thought it seemed to be getting brighter in the east. I went back and sat down beside the candle. I dozed again. Then I felt *sure* it was lighter in the east than it was in the west. I heard a bird begin to chirp. I opened my attache case and set the food on top of it, using it like a table. I took a knife and began to peel the wax from the cheese. But I couldn't see if I was getting just the wax or also some of the cheese. I knew I was rushing things a bit: it wasn't really light yet!

More birds began to chirp, and the east was brightening noticeably. The glow of the candle was not so obvious now—but it still was very much brighter than the space around it. It was now 5:15 a.m., and the sky got lighter with every passing minute. I took the blanket from around my shoulders, folded it in half, then into quarters, and then once more. I sat on the folded blanket, pulled the attache case in front of me—between me and the candle.

Birds were flying and singing all around me by 5:30 a.m., and it was very light. The glow from the candle had diminished until it didn't even light up the ground immediately around it. I stood up, and taking each item of food one at a time, I held it up in my right hand, raised my left hand in prayer and said: "Blessed are you, Lord, the God of all creation . . ." for each item. Those were happy prayers, accompanied by the singing of the birds. I sat on the blanket again. The orchard was bright; dawn was here. I broke the bread and began to eat.

The food and the wine were good—not terrific, but very good. I was grateful for the food, and careful not to drink too much of the wine. I had forgotten to bring a glass, so I had to drink from the bottle. The only thing which seemed not right was eating alone. Also, I was eating too fast, so I slowed down and tried to eat more reverently. Then I broke up part of the loaf and scattered it around the ground for the birds. That was so I wouldn't be eating alone.

I prayed a short prayer of thanks, and I felt sure that on this day when there was no celebration of the Eucharist, this was a good way to praise God. I corked the wine bottle, blew out the candle, put them back in the attache case. I picked up the blanket, folded it once more, put it under my arm and headed for the house. That night I wrote in my green book:

> I'm glad I did this. I'm glad it wasn't a great thrilling experience. It was nice, that's all. And I'm glad Peter wrote: "You can rely on the message of the prophets as something entirely trustworthy. Keep your eyes fixed on them. They are like a lamp burning in a dark place, until the Day dawns and the Morning Star rises in your heart." I'm glad this symbol entered my mind. I'm glad that after two years or more I finally made the symbol. I'm glad it wasn't all that terrific. And I'll probably do it again next Good Friday night.

> The talk went well at 10:15 a.m., even though I slept only from 6:30 to 9:45. I heard myself say some good things during the talk. I heard myself say: "Make symbols for yourself, and give yourself over to the symbols you make. But don't demand too much of your symbols. And don't get hooked on your symbols. They may serve to open you to the Spirit of God who is within you. They may help you tune him in. But he is God. It is God whom we seek, not our symbols." And again I knew I was speaking to myself. Or maybe the Spirit of God within me was speaking to me.

I take the time to tell you all this because it is an incident in my life which brings together not only a lot of different kinds of homemade (and unspectacular) symbols, but also because it shows my customary way of reacting to the urge I have to make symbols. I generalize to presume that a lot of others have been presented with the possibility of making some symbol in order to open the door to let God in; that I presume also others delay—as I do—in making the symbol which suggests itself; that they may finally get around to making their homemade symbol with varying degrees of satisfaction, and that they reflect later on the way they made themselves available to God in their symbol. All of us would probably benefit greatly if we didn't delay so long in making the symbols which suggest themselves.

The previous incident took place over a year ago. It stands out in my experience as one time when I combined all kinds of symbols which flowed rather spontaneously from inside of me. As I've reflected on the experience, I've recognized in this one incident many elements about which and with which symbols can be made if we use our creative religious imagination.

Fasting and eating became symbolic. The feeling of hunger and the activity of eating alone and with others was important. What I ate was significant to me, as well as how I ate. The ritual of preparing to eat was inspired partly by familiarity with a tradition of praying and partly by my spontaneous urge to do so before I began to eat.

Posture was a part of it all: standing, sitting, kneeling. So were the gestures: walking, raising my arms, holding up the food. Light and darkness, sleeping and keeping awake, words, hearing, speaking, tasting, seeing, touching, the hours of the night—these were all symbolic in ways I can't even articulate. The place I chose was significant, and so was the time. Above all, the scripture passage which inspired the whole event was symbolic.

I think nearly all of us experience the urge to make symbols in our attempts to make ourselves available to God in prayer. There are, of course, great religious traditions which have made rites and rituals to aid individuals and gatherings in their prayer. But beyond these systematized symbolic openings, our spirits seek expression in unique symbolic ways. If we pay attention to these urges and give vent to them, our sense of personal prayer could increase. Often we will draw, no doubt, on the religious traditions which have shaped our spiritual outlook, and we will do so spontaneously. At other times we will manufacture entirely new expressions of who and how we are as we come before the Lord.

One night, very late, I was talking with a young man. We had talked of spiritual life and of our beliefs. We had both spoken of our recognition for the need to pray long, and so, even though it was late, we decided to pray before we went to bed. We sat on the floor and lit a candle. We prayed silently for a while; then we both verbalized some of our prayer. After a long period of silent prayer, he said he'd like to join hands and pray together the Lord's Prayer. We did so.

After finishing the Our Father, he grasped my hands quite tightly, and then released them. He did this several times. I asked him what this meant, and he said something vague about holding on, but being able to let go of the secure feeling and drift off.

Then he spread his arms wide like the wings of a bird in flight. I asked him what he was symbolizing. He said he was flying forward, but that his head was turned around. He pointed to his neck and said, "The trouble is here. I'm flying, but I'm looking back." I asked if he could tell me what it was he didn't want to leave behind, but he couldn't see what it was.

He moved a bit restlessly and lowered his back to the floor. "I feel like I'm falling," he said. "But I have no fear of crashing or of being hurt." I asked if he was in touch with God. He said he was. When he next verbalized his prayer, it was one of trustfulness.

We prayed together for some time longer and then we went off to our rooms. The next day we talked about our prayer and the symbols we had made. He knew that he was having an interior struggle with letting go of something familiar, and by simply letting himself make the gestures, which came to him spontaneously, he had opened the door to allow his God in. He had been touched and moved by God.

Praying is about making space and making symbols. We are the symbol-makers. We learn some symbols and use them in our praying; others spring from us spontaneously as we try to open the door to allow God into ourselves as we really are. There is benefit and perhaps even need for each person to create homemade symbols—symbols of doubt as well as of faith, symbols of woundedness as well as of healing, symbols of disappointment as well as of joy. Making symbols of who and how we are is probably more important for prayer than simply understanding the particular way we happen to be.

If you would pray, make your own symbols.

6. Words Are Symbols

Our words are not homemade; they are a product of the culture in which we have been raised. We can choose the words we use, and with the words we use we can give expression to our person. But even the most carefully chosen words used to express the most personal of interior experiences are laden with meanings and a history we may not suspect. The words we use embody fragments of the cultural past which spawned the words. This past may be forgotten by the current user of the words, but it remains enshrined in the words themselves.

If we can take the time to get in touch with the words we choose, and if we can see what personal history is expressed by the simple choice of our words, we can see more clearly the tradition we bring to bear on our present experience.

There are three levels to everything we say or write: the immediate level, or the personal reality; the personal historical level which has given us the particular words we use; and the cultural traditional level which has given to the words we use a meaning and nuance which may escape us altogether. By speaking or writing about our experience, therefore, we automatically interpret that experience in the light of our personal history and our cultural tradition. The experience is ours, but we use our personal history and our cultural tradition to interpret it.

One February afternoon I was talking with a young black man about his experience of ministry within his church. He was about to request ordination to the diaconate, and was reflecting on what he had experienced during the past five years in teaching religion in a high school run by his denomination. He had also been involved in social ministry and, to some extent, in preaching and counseling.

A significant part of his reflections centered on the frustration he had experienced—frustration arising from the lack of success in what he had undertaken, and frustration from dealing with the administration of his predominantly white church.

He had often felt that he was misunderstood. Now he was thinking that perhaps his lack of appreciation for the difficulty others had in understanding his experience had caused part of the problem. I asked him why he even considered committing himself to a life of ministry in the organization which had occasioned so much frustration. He leaned back in his chair and said, "Well, Keith, I see the whole church as a group of people struggling and moving on. Some get tired and fall down—never to get up again. Others fall and are helped to get up by other tired people who plod on. It's a group of very imperfect people trying their best to arrive at where they want to be."

I asked him, "Where are you getting those words and images you just used to talk about your experience of ministry?"

He said they came from his mother and grandmother. His mother struggled against alcoholism all her life, and his grandmother, his mother's mother, would always encourage her. When she fell, Grandmother would always be there to pick her up and take care of the family while her daughter recovered from her latest bout with the bottle. Grandmother herself had some problems with alcohol. But somehow, despite her own difficulties, Grandmother was able to hold the family together. Often Grandmother would wonder with her grandchildren, "What will happen when I'm gone?" When the mother died suddenly, Grandmother was still there, still believing, still struggling with her own weakness and with keeping the family together.

As we continued to talk about the young man's experience of ministry and his proposed commitment to the diaconate, and as we reflected on the personal history which shaped his perception of his present experience, the Exodus event emerged clearly as the religious and spiritual model from which he drew the words to describe his present life and his personal history. As he talked I could almost see the Israelities struggling across a desert land, falling at times—sometimes exhausted, sometimes sinful—then getting up again, and continuing on in the hope of someday reaching the Promised Land.

All of us are shaped by our personal history. And that personal history is shaped by spiritual and religious traditions. These traditions have influenced our perception of life, and we maintain and continue them and apply them to entirely new situations. We are both the product and the developers of an ongoing religious and spiritual tradition. Our words help us to recognize the tradition which has shaped us and which we continue to develop.

Words are symbols. They are symbols which we make, often without adverting to their meaning. If we train ourselves to hear what words we use—whether we speak them out loud, or groan them within our spirits, or write them—we can get in touch with our traditions.

How can we identify which traditions are shaping our approach to life? For me, the surest way to externalize the content of my spirit is to write. In writing I am able to examine the verbal symbols I use to help me make sense

out of life. When I write down my thoughts and feelings
—or simply the descriptions of events about which I have
thoughts and feelings—the words I choose concretize my
life story, so that I can see what I am saying to myself about
my life. In reading the words I use to speak about my life,
I can identify the traditions that have shaped my perceptions. Then I can enter more explicitly into those traditions. I can nourish my spirit more fully on the sources
from which it springs and draws its life.

The young black man who contemplated ordination
to the diaconate found, in the words he used to describe his
frustration, the spiritual and religious tradition from which
he drew his strength to meet those frustrations. It was
the tradition of the Exodus journey. Once this was clear
to him, he could more easily make himself available to the
God who had revealed himself to an ancient people in
events similar to those which confronted him today. In his
reflection on his own life's experiences, he was further
developing the faith with which that ancient people had
responded to the timeless God. The young deacon-to-be
ministered to his people, not only in the service he ren-
dered, but also as a theologian making explicit for his
people the revelation of their God to them.

For more years than I care to think about, I was
urged by spiritual directors and teachers to write out accounts of the events of my day. I was assured that there
was in this practice some significant benefit for my spiritual
growth. Once or twice I began a notebook with the descrip-
tion of some incident and my reactions to it, only to tear
out the single page months later to use the notebook for
another purpose.

One day, as part of a workshop I was participating in,
I was asked to write up a "critical incident" of the recent
past for the sake of reflecting theologically on it. I did so,
not believing much could come from it. Before the workshop was over, though, I was convinced of the value of
writing. I've written almost daily ever since. Many times

I begin with the conviction that I really have nothing to write about. Sometimes I start off with a line like, "I don't know why I'm writing tonight. I have nothing on my mind." Then I just keep writing. In reading over my accumulated meanderings, I have often found significant directions taking shape in my life without my being aware of them. Once I become aware of them and of the source of the reflections I find within myself, I can enter more fully and more freely into the sources from which I have been drawing my strength unconsciously.

I know this sounds very theoretical. Let me tell you how I first realized the benefit of watching the words I used to symbolize my experiences. One day in March, 1976, I wrote the following in my green book:

> I have been wondering what I should write up as my critical incident for the theological reflection workshop in a week. I have been looking back on past experiences, but this morning I began looking ahead.
>
> For the past two months I have known that Sister Clarissima, Brother Conrad's niece, has been in the hospital with terminal cancer. Fr. Alexis told me, and I said I'd visit her. Then a sister from her community told me about her, and I promised to visit, but I haven't done so yet.
>
> I have felt uncomfortable about it. I don't know her very well, and I feel funny about going to see her when she is dying. The main motives I have for going to see her are that Fr. Alexis and Sister Mary Lou think I should. It hasn't been care for Sister Clarissima which prompts me to go.
>
> However, I did decide yesterday to go. And this morning while I was shaving, I recalled the words of the Gospel about visiting the sick and Jesus' words, "Whatever you do. . ."
>
> Then I found inside of me something I want to say to her. I want to tell her I'm glad I

met her. I guess it has been so important to me to know a visit from me would mean something to her (and I haven't been sure it would), that I haven't been willing to take the initiative to do something *for her*. So now I leave and go to visit her.

At that point I stopped writing and drove the 20 miles or so to the town where she was hospitalized. When I returned home, I continued to write:

I went into her room; her blood sister and another sister from her religious community were in the room. Sister Clarissima was sleeping (she had been heavily sedated earlier). She stirred a bit as I introduced myself to the other two women. I spoke briefly to Sister Clarissima, telling her who I was. I told her I had come just to thank her for her contribution to my life—a couple of very bright spots in my life.

Her sister filled me in on the whole illness. Cancer discovered over a year ago. Surgery. Recovery. More surgery. Blood poisoning. Recovery. And a month ago, a relapse—recognized even then as the end.

The end of her life here on earth is close, apparently. I gave her my blessing, again thanked her for what she gave to me, asked the other two if they had eaten lunch yet—they said, "Yes"—gave them my name and address, and left.

As I started the car, I realized that my reluctance in going to see her was because I was not sure I had anything to give her which she might want. And I didn't want to go empty-handed. I wanted to go to her with a gift—something which gave me strength and wealth. I did not want to go helpless and in poverty. So when I could bring a word of thanks which was genuine, I was able to go. But my going was good, not because of the gift I brought, but because I,

another helpless and poor human being, went to
a sister human being whose helplessness and poverty differ from mine only in that hers is more
obvious to most people.

I'm glad I went. I'm glad I gave her my
word of thanks. In giving her that I recognized
my own indebtedness to her, and therefore my
own weakness and poverty. That was her gift
to me. And I thank her and God for that.

In this writing I recorded the incident—the simple
facts—and my reaction to those facts. I thought that I
had exhausted the possibilities of the event. But when I
brought that writing to the workshop, the leader asked me
to look at the words I had used to describe the incident
and the words I had used to record my reaction to the
incident. As I looked at the *words,* now, and not just at the
thoughts I had tried to express through them, I had a
whole new realization.

I am a Franciscan. Part of the religious tradition
which has formed me is the Franciscan tradition. When I
looked at the words I had used to describe that day in
March when I went to visit a dying sister, I discovered that
I had used words similar and even identical to words and
phrases in the rule of Saint Francis and in some other of his
writings. He wrote: "Serving the Lord in poverty and
humility, dearest brothers, let us go seeking alms with
confidence. Nor ought we to be ashamed, since for our sakes
our Lord while on earth made himself poor in this world."

I had read that phrase many times in my life, and it
had in some ways formed my spiritual and religious outlook. But until I looked closely at the words I had chosen
to relate an event in 1976, I hadn't grasped the meaning
of those words in 1223. Only then did I see the connec-
tion with the words and faith spelled out twelve centuries
earlier: "Though he was in the form of God, he did not
deem equality with God something to be grasped at.
Rather he emptied himself and took the form of a slave,

being born in human likeness. And he was known to be of human estate."

In coming to recognize how my present perception of events was shaped by my personal history, and how my personal history was shaped by the spiritual and religious traditions which formed me, I could freely and consciously open myself to further growth in that tradition. I could ask to be made poor and humble because I now saw the beauty of it. I was open to what the Lord might want to do.

Words are symbols—symbols we make in our attempt to open the door to allow our God to enter our lives. If we allow ourselves to choose the words which suggest themselves as we stew over our lives, and if we advert to the words we use, we are more able to hear him knocking and to open the door. If, however, we deny ourselves the freedom to choose our own words—our own style of speaking—and select only "proper" words and the "correct" style, we may never discover the depth of faith which is within us. Our own words spoken or thought or written in our own style are homemade symbols through which we make ourselves available to God.

Let me give you an example of what NOT to do. I was approaching the office of a man who was considering going with me to a convention. As I raised my hand to knock on his door, I heard him say, "Damn! I just can't afford it!" I knocked, was invited in and we talked about whether or not he was going to attend the convention. Finally he said, "I won't be able to go; the cost is prohibitive."

"The cost is prohibitive," is a far cry from "Damn! I just can't afford it!" I was knocking at his door. The man said, "Come in." But what I had heard through the door was not what he said when I was standing in front of him, face to face. When he was talking to me, he chose proper words and a correct style.

If he were to reflect on his experience at that moment, by writing down his words and examining them, he'd get much more insight into himself if he reflected on "Damn! I just can't afford it!" than he would if he spent days looking at "The cost is prohibitive."

The same is true of the words we use in praying. When we open the door to let him in, it's probably a mistake to "clean up our act." Much more of our spirit is expressed in the kinds of words we spontaneously choose.

If you care to try writing as a way to become aware of the word-symbols you spontaneously make, I suggest the following method:

Record as fully as you can remember them the facts or the data of the event you are considering. It should be an event which engages you personally—either because you took part in it, or because it in some other way touches you.

Then record your reaction to that data. Did you have any particular emotional response? Did the incident evoke from you some insistence on principles you hold dear? Did your reaction clarify any attitudes you hold habitually? Write it all out just as it comes to your mind. Don't edit.

Then look at the words and phrases you've used. Where do they come from? Are you aware of any source —from your own personal history or from some religious or spiritual tradition—which has shaped and influenced your choice of words?

If you can discover the source of the words you've used, you are now consciously aware of the religious or spiritual or theological tradition which has shaped your perception of life; you can be open to be further shaped in that faith. Because you have brought the richness of that tradition to bear on your experience, you have advanced the development of that tradition, applying it to a new situation—a situation which never existed before. Such application develops and clarifies the very faith-tradition which interprets the new reality.

This process will take time—space, if you wish. And it may yield no immediate results that are perceivable or rewarding. But I've come to believe that, for me, there is significant benefit to be found in writing. The words I choose are symbols I make. Most of them are homemade. These symbols have helped me open the door to allow him in on me just as I am.

If you would pray, make space, make symbols.

7. Faithful to My Symbols

The town was still small enough that everyone knew everybody else—and knew just about everything about everybody else. This wasn't considered a bad thing; the townsfolk liked it that way. When Joses and his wife and young son moved to town from the hills around Tabor just a few miles to the north, everyone knew he was sick. His cousins had invited him and his family to live with them, since he could no longer herd his sheep.

Actually, everyone in Naim knew Joses was going to die. He didn't breathe right. But his wife took care of him, and he got about town for almost a year and a half. Only when his wife was walking in the market or when the couple came to the synagogue did anyone bother to pretend that Joses was going to live through the winter. And he didn't.

That was last winter. Joses had made a journey to Jerusalem in the caravan of people from Galilee the spring before he died. His son had come of age, and it was time for him to meet and be taught by the doctors of the Law in the temple, and to take his place among the men in the synagogue at home. But Joses, worn out by the journey, took seriously ill in the fall and died.

81

His son grew to be 15 years old. Everyone said he was the image of his father. When he read in the synagogue it was spooky. He spoke with just a trace of the raspy voice which was his father's.

He had taken up his father's trade, but continued to live with his mother in town. He wasn't a strong lad, but he was determined and dependable. When he took sick, nothing much was made of it. His mother nursed him, hoping for a quick recovery because when he was home he was a big help to her. She didn't even consider the possibility that he might die. She just wanted to be rid of the inconvenience his illness caused her.

Then the sickness worsened, and the woman began to know fear. Now she hoped for recovery with much more intensity, and now her hope was not so selfish. Still, she felt panic—and anger at God: how could he threaten her with another tragic loss of one she loved? As the illness grew worse and her efforts more frantic, hope began to slip away. This morning the boy had died, and her hope had died along with her son. In her grief, she still had to face the reality which confronted her. Anger at God disappeared; it was replaced by a disbelieving question, "Why?"

Nothing remained now but to play out the drama. Throughout the day there would be the mourning, and then the burial. The widow's heart bore the burden of sadness, loss, guilt over her selfish hope at the beginning of the illness and guilt over her anger at God. But she accepted her helpless and sinful state and proceeded with the rituals and necessities. Life—her life—must go on, though she wasn't sure why.

The mourning at the bedside over, the preparations completed, it was time for the burial. And then the appearance of the strangers coming toward the city gate as the funeral procession moved out toward the cemetery. The leader of the group of strangers didn't take the opportunity to slip by the crowd, but moved right into it—right up to the stretcher. When he touched it the bearers stopped.

What could the man want? If he was looking for trouble he had chosen the wrong group. Over half the town was here.

He looked at the mother. "Don't cry," he said. But what a strange and awful thing to say. Memories of past hopes welled up. She had not wanted to cry; she had hoped to avoid altogether this occasion which caused her tears. But the worst had happened, and with her hope gone, nothing was left but to cry. She had hoped. God knew, she had hoped. But now tears were her only hope, her only salvation.

The stranger spoke. "Young man, I tell you to get up."

What terrible words! Words which challenged the obvious reality of the situation. Words which had to be a mockery—or the most powerful words ever spoken! Hope glimmered so very faintly. And that glimmer was resented. Why allow hope to be rekindled? But hope did glow — oh, so very faintly.

The dead man sat up and began to speak! The stranger took the young man's hand and placed it in his mother's. Then he turned his face again toward the city gate.

My personal appreciation of the widow of Naim's plight came at a time in my life when I was feeling like Job. I wasn't suffering any particular hardships myself, but it seemed that each time the phone rang I was informed of the struggles and tragedies of those I loved. Each caller might have ended with, "And I alone escaped to tell thee." One night, after stewing over all these happenings in prayer, I opened the scripture and came to the story of the widow of Naim. I wrote in my green book:

> I am that mother. Past tragedies have been endured and current ones are not recognized as being all that serious. Surely the illness will pass. It's only an inconvenience I am asked to put up with. At most it's an annoyance. But it worsens. Panic! Anger! Disbelief! and then acceptance of

the inevitable. On with the rituals; on with the necessities which living demands. It's over. Hope dies.

But there is One whose word mocks the tragedy of life. One whose word does not describe what is in reality, but defines what shall be real! And to me he's a stranger. I ask only that he pass by this way to say, "Don't cry!"

Lord, help me trust the power of your word and the greatness of your compassion.

I went to bed much consoled by my reflections on the widow of Naim and by the Lord. I had stewed and reflected and prayed, and I felt better. The next morning I woke up and almost immediately wrote in my green book:

I just woke up, and I opened this book again. It now seems to me that in the incident of the widow of Naim hope is not what is called for. "Abandon" came to mind, and I wanted to dismiss it from my mind. It seems too quietist. It seems as though we are called to be more active in shaping our destiny. But it wouldn't go away. After we've hoped and worked, and seen all our hoping and working go for naught, we are called to trust in the Lordship of Jesus over the events we have experienced and to entrust ourselves to him by abandoning ourselves to the events. Surely they have escaped our dominion, but not his.

Had the widow not abandoned herself to the rituals and the necessities of life, she would not have been at the gates of the city as Jesus passed by. She would have been home denying, or at least failing to enter into the events which had shaped her life. She would never have heard him say, "Don't cry," nor would she have experienced the power of his word which made crying unnecessary and unwarranted.

For me the widow of Naim is a model of faithfulness to ritual, faithfulness to symbol. Sometimes life seems too tragic or too boring to symbolize in prayer. Sometimes I'd rather just stay home and let it pass by. Sometimes I'm too sinful, too busy, too tired, too preoccupied to enter into life as it is. I don't want to continue with the rituals of praying, because they have become so meaningless, or so routine, or so unexciting, or so painful. But the widow, whose name I don't even know, invites me to go on, to continue to make symbols expressive of precisely who and how I am. And he will pass by.

In scripture the phrase "to pass by" always means a revelation of God to an individual or a group. I think of bringing myself to prayer very much like the widow bringing herself, just as she was, to the city gate. Jesus is going to pass by this way. If, because I'm too tired or too full of pizza, or too horny or too preoccupied or too bored, I don't bring myself to prayer, I'll never be there to hear him speak the word of power to heal or strengthen or uplift me. Prayer—and faithfulness to prayer—brings us to the city gate as he passes by, as he reveals himself.

Sometimes praying is enchanting. Occasionally it is exciting. At some periods of my life I am driven to it by pressures and panic. But most of life is lived, not on the mountain peaks and not in the valleys, but on the plains. Nothing about life on the plains entices or demands prayer. If I pray, it is because I believe in the good of it. If I wait for the excitement or the disaster to bring me to prayer, I won't pray on the plains. There are so many other things to occupy my time and attention on the plains, things exciting and things worrisome.

If ever there was a person who would have been excused from going on with the rituals and necessities of life, it was the widow of Naim. Yet she carried on. Her faithfulness to the symbols invites me to a similar faithfulness.

Prayer is like eating. We eat day in and day out, hardly noticing the menu or making any fuss over the quality of the food we eat. But we eat! We're accustomed to eating certain things at certain times in certain ways. When we're excited or anguished, our eating habits change. We forget to eat. We eat too fast. We eat more than we should, or less than normal. So, too, in praying—times of weariness, of trouble, of excitement, may make our prayer more picky. The valleys and the mountain peaks definitely affect the appetite!

Praying has become a very important grace in my life; but faithfulness to praying is a gift over and above the grace of prayer. I'm not always faithful to praying, but more and more I see that my moments of not being faithful are mountaintop or valley-depth moments. I don't worry about this nearly as much as I would worry if the space and symbols of praying were missing from my normal routine.

When a person finds the space—or makes it—and discovers the kinds of symbols which make him or her available to God, that space and those symbols become something like the meeting tent described in the Old Testament. Even though the Israelites were a people who were sometimes wandering, sometimes on a journey to a definite destination, they always carried with them the meeting tent. Every time they pitched camp, they set up the meeting tent. There Moses and the elders entered into God's presence to receive direction and instruction for the Israelite community.

Moses had first met God on a mountain in a burning bush. Later the Israelites experienced the presence of God on Mount Sinai. Previous to these powerful mountaintop experiences of God they had their valley-depth experiences in Egypt—where their prayer was one of anguish. In the valley of pain and on the mountain of ecstasy they made themselves available to God—praying for deliverance from their weakness and woundedness or pledging their obedience. But on the plains—in the desert—they forgot their dependence on God and their experience of his majesty.

Always in their midst was the meeting tent. The ritual of setting it up and taking it down was, no doubt, a nuisance

at times. But it was the symbol of what and who they were,
a people chosen and led by God. By faithfulness to the
ritual they remained available to be touched and moved by
the God they had met in the valley and on the mountain.

Our own personal symbols, as well as those of our
religious tradition, are like the meeting tent which the
Israelites set up each time they made their camp. It was a
nuisance—the work of keeping the meeting tent among
them—but they were faithful to it.

The symbols we use to make ourselves available to
God to be touched and moved by him, the symbols we use
to open the door for him to come in to us as we are, are
as important for us as the meeting tent was for the Israelites. These symbols may have been discovered in some
mountaintop or some valley experience when we were driven
to make them out of desperation or prompted to make them
by our elation. But on the plains of our routine living these
same symbols—or others—assure us that we are God's
people and that we receive the direction for our journey
from him. Faithfulness to symbol-making on the plains is
important for growth and progress in our journey.

Are symbols, therefore, forever? No. We have to learn
when to let go of a particular symbol, a particular way of
praying. But the time never arrives to stop praying altogether. A particular symbol may no longer serve to make
us available to God, because we've changed. But if we are
faithful to praying and continue our attempts to allow him
to come in to us as we really are, we will be led to make
new symbols and to let go of familiar ones. Faithfulness to
making symbols is not a matter of superstition. God is not
in the symbol; the symbol we make is not God. Every
symbol—every form of praying—is good insofar as it
serves to make us available to God to be touched and
moved by him. When it no longer serves that purpose, it
should be laid aside to be replaced by another symbol which
is expressive of who and how we are now.

A year after my very moving experience of the all-night vigil on Good Friday, I found myself in the same location, and I decided to do the same thing again. I began the day in the same way—fasting from solid food—and prepared to spend the night outside, waiting for dawn. However, Good Friday was two weeks earlier in the season than it had been the previous year, and it was about 20 degrees cooler! I sat up very late in my room, and about three o'clock in the morning I knew I was doing this only because it *had been* so meaningful the previous year. This year it was not something which came from my sense of making myself available to God; it was only a return to a former symbol—a symbol which did nothing for me now. So at 3:00 a.m. I said good night and went to bed.

A particular symbol's usefulness may come to an end, but to be without symbols—to cease praying—would be to decide to eat only in moments when panic or ecstasy prompts us. The length of the time periods between my panic or ecstatic moments would guarantee that I'd starve to death if that were the only time I nourished my spirit, if that were the only time I prayed. Prayer on the plains is necessary.

There was a widow who had just lost her only son. The tragedy was seen by everyone as more than enough to excuse her from going to the cemetery with the procession carrying her boy's body. But she went on with the ritual— on with life. And she was there when he passed by.

If you would pray, make space, make symbols, and be faithful about it.

8. Reclaiming Lost Space

"But what if I haven't been faithful to making space, making symbols? How do I begin again? Do I wait for another panic or ecstatic experience to initiate my praying and continue from there? Or is there a way I can begin again simply because I choose to begin?"

Occasionally I meet people who ask those kinds of questions. Usually the question is more veiled than that, and often it isn't in the form of a question. A 25-year-old junior executive of a small company who is sitting beside me in an airplane says, "I was raised a Catholic, but we stopped going to church shortly after we got married. Now our son is three and I feel like there's something we should be doing for him in terms of his religious education. I'm not sure we can do it."

A young priest, ordained three years and receiving some acclaim from the parishioners of a suburban parish, says he's starting to feel a little hypocritical when he preaches his sermon on the first Sunday of Lent. "I told them that Lent is a time of conversion to prayer and

penance and praying the scriptures and renewal of our
service to our neighbors. The service to others sounds OK
to me, but I'm not sure where I am with the prayer bit."

A college sophomore coed writes to her mother after
she returns to school from Christmas vacation: "Mom, I felt
like a hypocrite while I was home. I haven't been going to
church on Sunday for almost a year. I just don't believe all
that stuff anymore like I used to. When I come home for
semester break I just won't be able to go to church with you
and Dad and the kids. I hope you understand, Mom. I know
you will; you always do. But please don't say I'm just going
through a phase. This is really how I feel."

A 52-year-old man, recovering nicely from serious
surgery, tells the pastoral minister of the hospital that he's
happy and grateful to everyone who was with him during
the past week. Then he adds, "I feel like I should be
thanking God and getting my life a little more religious. But
it's been so long."

I hear all these people saying somewhat the same
thing: either their symbols failed them or they were not
faithful to their symbols. Many people live their lives remembering a time when praying made sense, both the
formal religious rituals into which they were indoctrinated
and the space and symbols they were taught or discovered
on their own for personal prayer. But for so many this is a
thing of the past, something that has ceased to be meaningful. Most of the people I've talked with don't regret that
there was such a time in their past, but they don't see it as
real for them now. They don't see it as bad . . . just past,
outgrown, laid aside, left behind. This "not bad, just past"
feeling makes me think they are really asking if it is possible
and sensible for them to start again. A lot of other things
in their past are regretted, but seldom do they regret having
prayed.

It doesn't surprise me that the symbols we've learned
or the ones we've designed eventually disappoint us. They
were learned or devised to be expressive of who we were

and how we knew ourselves to be. But we grew and changed.

Think, for example, of the first symbols we learned. We learned them through mimicry, just as we learned all things through mimicry. The big people in our world showed us how to do them. They were in some cases very accurate expressions of our relationship to God, but they were designed to be grasped and entered into with a child's feelings and imagination. As we grew a little older, our symbols became inadequate. They expressed the same realities, but we were no longer the same person with the same perceptions. When we were taught new symbols or encouraged to find new ones for ourselves, we could lay aside the first ones gracefully and continue to indulge in symbol-making.

This experience of transition and of growth happens many times in one's life. Sometimes it occurs at predictable stages; at other times because personal awarenesses and perceptions change. Some time-honored rituals are expressive of eternally valid stances of humankind before God, but we still perceive them in the time-bound situation of the day we learned them. We often assume that what we experienced then exhausted the meaning of the symbols we used. We have lost respect for our symbols, and they are easily laid aside when we change. We have not been helped to see their meaning for our new experiences.

Perhaps when we broke off with making space and making symbols, we felt our lives to be more real. Yet I suspect there remains some mild hankering for that world which disintegrated.

Respect means literally "to look again." What we lost and might want to reclaim is the willingness to look again at those symbols which we thought had yielded up all their meaning to the devout children we once were. Perhaps now they will yield more meaning for the persons we know ourselves to be today.

I have often heard the story of a young man who was

raised on a farm and then left home to enjoy a more extravagant and refined life. He ended up out of contact with his family, working on another farm because the kind of city life he got mixed up in took all his money and disappointed him. He knew his father wouldn't approve of the kind of work he was doing: his dad raised crops, but he was working for a man in the livestock business. And that wasn't all his father would disapprove! He would be shocked to know how the money his son had taken with him was spent, and more horrified still to see where his son's reckless living had landed him.

The Prodigal Son has gotten a lot of bad press over the years, but what he did seems quite normal. He had been going through all the rituals ever since he was old enough to work in his father's fields. At first it was fun to be introduced into the rituals of his older brother and the hired hands. His father had personally showed him how to sow and to reap.

But he reached a day in his life when he decided there had to be more to life than he was seeing. He felt confined by the narrow existence which was his and his family's. So he asked for the wherewithal to set out on his own. Dad had ignored him at first, then argued with him, and then gave in. But he knew he didn't like the whole venture.

At first, life in the real world was exciting: Money could buy almost anything, and almost anything was available. He hardly ever thought of home, but when he did it was with disdain. How had he allowed himself to be so narrow and so confined? It hadn't been too bad while he was there, but he knew he could never go back now. He didn't think that way anymore, and neither did his new friends.

But here, beside the pigpen, he wasn't so sure. His new friends left as soon as his money ran out. When he had exhausted every other possibility, the lad had looked up one of these "friends" to ask for a loan to help him get back on his feet. But his friend was essentially a businessman like his father, and he had said no. He did get his father to hire him, though. So here he sat. No food, no money, no clothes, no sandals. His own father, he remembered, paid the hired hands every sundown. He didn't even know when he would get paid for working here. Ah, the real world!

He thought back to what he had left. He recalled exactly how he had lived, but he felt differently about it now than he had when he left home. He knew he couldn't go back to what had been before. Innocence was gone. But maybe he could reclaim something of his early life experience. He could take up the rituals again—rising early and heading out to the fields, not to return till nightfall. A lunch to take along and a skin of wine always ready when he got up. He couldn't go back to taking those things for granted as he once had. He could hardly reclaim his position as a child in the family, but he could work. He could be one of the laborers on his father's farm.

He kicked the nearest sow and bounded over the fence. "Where are you going?" asked a worker as indigent as himself. "Home!" he answered, and he didn't believe the sound of the word in his own ears.

Home wouldn't be the same; it couldn't be the same. He didn't want it to be the same. He recalled how it had been. He was younger then, and more naive. He thought over the events of the past two years: the times he was robbed; the people who helped him and those who only pretended to help; the drinking and the orgies; the time he fell into a dry gulch when he was drunk. It's a miracle he wasn't killed.

He slept that night in a field and walked the whole next day. It was going to be embarrassing to look his father in the eye. What would he say to him? Well, at least his dad might be surprised and even glad he was still alive. And as he raced through the events of the past two years, he actually found himself surprised and glad he was still alive. He cried hot tears, not for sorrow, but for joy and gratitude. He was going home.

For the Prodigal Son, it was a depressing experience

which made him return home. For other people it is a joyful happening. For still others it is a simple matter of deciding to go home. Whatever the impetus, the process of reclaiming lost space is similar. It is the process of remembering—not just thinking back on how it was when one used to pray, but recalling the events of the intervening years.

When we break off making space and making symbols, we tend to feel as if we are taking our lives into our own hands. We set out to be the producer/director of a film in which we star. If we look at the events which have made up our lives, at the people we've met who have influenced us for good or for ill, we may find that most of our lives is not the product of our own doing. We are not the producer/director nearly so much as we are the product. No matter how free we know ourselves to be in making choices, a large segment of our life is not choosable. The events and people we have not chosen to come into contact with have shaped our lives more than have our own choices.

If we're not the producer/director, who is?

God is. Jesus is Lord of every event of human history, and he has dominion over those events, even our free choices.

Memory is the way to reclaim lost space. If we will remember back to a time when we made space and symbols, when doing so made sense to us, we can link up with our roots. Then by recalling in as great a detail as we can the intervening events and people who have shaped our life to bring us to where we are today, we can come to know of the One who is indeed the Producer/Director of the person we have become. Each of us can say with surprise and gladness, "It's a miracle I'm still alive!"

I had an extraordinarily deep experience of gratitude on a retreat once. The man who was directing the retreat passed out a slip of paper and said that we could use it if we felt so inclined, but he said we shouldn't let it get in the way of our reflecting and praying. I took the page to my room after his talk and laid it on my desk. I forgot about it until the following afternoon. I picked it up and read it. And then I did what it suggested. I'm going to share that page with you. If you care to reclaim lost space in your own life I suggest you spend several hours on the following project.

Tape together several pages of blank paper until you have a length of paper as many inches long as there are years in your life up to this point. On the lower edge of the pages draw a line representing your life from conception to the present. Divide the line into inch-long segments, each section representing one year of your life. On the rest of the space note significant events in which the Father's goodness made its appearance to you—through persons, events and things. At the time they may have seemed like nothing special, or even like tragedies, but now you can see those events, persons and things as blessings.

Include such things as the circumstances surrounding your conception and birth, if you know about them, and those surrounding your naming; people who entered your life significantly at various points—friends, family, enemies, chance acquaintances; painful experiences which bore unexpected and even unrecognized fruits; unexplained happenings; unexpected joys; "accidents"; ordinary happenings which you remember without understanding why you remember them; illnesses.

Simply jot in names and brief descriptions on the pages above the line and draw arrows to the point on the line representing the time in which they occurred.

Then look over your life-line. Do not try to understand all the particular meanings that may have gone unrecognized up to this point. Simply allow the total reality of your life to affect you. Remember fully any persons or events which may particularly catch your attention. Do you see any connections that you never saw before? Having reclaimed this space, symbolize how and who you are *now*. How do you respond to this glimpse into your life? Grateful? Fearful? Resentful? Symbolize in words, gestures, posture, how this experience of contemplating your life affects you.

This is not an exercise only for those who have stopped praying. It can help reclaim lost space for anyone who takes praying seriously, and it provides a deep sense of returning home.

I remember the very first time someone asked me to teach him to pray. I went for a walk with that young man, and I asked him to lead me to a place which he found congenial, a place where he felt at home. He led me to the base of a huge tree and he sat down. We were quiet for a few minutes. Then I asked him, "Is there anything you would like to say to your Father?"

I told him not to say it out loud, but simply to look WITHIN and to become aware of what was INSIDE himself which he wanted to say.

Then, after many minutes of silence, I asked him, "Is there anything you would like your Father to say to you?"

Again, I wanted him to listen to the depths of his own spirit, because the Spirit of God has been united to our own spirit in the cry we make. It was simply a way to make the space necessary for the prayer of the Spirit to emerge.

I went inside then and left him alone. About half an hour later he walked by my office and said, "Thanks."

If you would pray, reclaim your lost space and return home to your Father.

9. Surveying the Land

I began this book by considering the need to clear the land, to make space outside ourselves in which we could pray. Only enough space is required that our own spirit can be quiet and alone long enough to hear him knocking.

But now I'm thinking of "land" in another sense.

Several months after I gave that retreat to the seminarians in Denver, I returned to that city for a convention. After the convention ended I spent three days at the seminary. Three of the men took me to the mountains as they had promised they would if ever I got back to Denver.

All three of them had been at the seminary for three and a half years, and each had his own favorite place in the mountains. I was going to get a tour to all these places in one day. We left at nine o'clock on Saturday morning, stopped at a grocery store to buy bagels, cream cheese and a bottle of wine. Then into the hills.

We drove to several peaks and passes. Each time we stopped the car we got out and hiked, once around a small mountain lake, another time overlooking another lake—there we ate our bagels and drank our wine. Again we stopped at Loveland Pass, which we had intended to climb, but the wind was too cold and blowing too hard.

Twice I remember feeling as if I were standing on the highest spot in the world. Everything there was to see was beneath us, except for the puffy clouds in the sky. The guys said it was the clearest day they could remember. From one mountain we looked down on the little town of Georgetown and the valley which stretched off into the distance. From Squaw Pass, I believe it was, we looked down on a mountain meadow below, and beyond the mountains we could see out to the plains east of Denver.

The seminarians had taken me to their special places in the mountains and from those spots we viewed the valleys below. From the top of the mountain or the hill we could see and recognize, at times, where we had been or where we were going next.

I'd like to conclude this book by recalling the idea of "land" in this sense: from our mountaintops we could survey the land. We could see the road and the terrain below. We had come up the mountain from down there, but it was only from "up here" that we could get a perspective on where we had been or where we were going.

While praying—making space and making symbols— is a very personal endeavor, there is a danger that we will clear our own little portion of land and never see it in relationship to the whole panorama of the world. Even our concern with such a worthwhile endeavor as being available to our God can become a narrow concern. That is, of course, a mistake and something unfortunate, because the God to whom we seek to be available is the God to whom all our brothers and sisters in this world also pray. Whatever the circumstances of our lives, there are others who share our world, others whose circumstances are of equal importance to our one God. No matter how alone I become in order to pray, I'm not alone in prayer itself.

The God to whom I make myself available in my praying has revealed that he is concerned about the plight of all his people. Presumably, if I make myself available to him to be touched and moved by him, he is going to touch me with his concern for his people and move me to make those concerns my own.

The more I pray, the more I'm going to become concerned with the sinful condition of my world, and with the saving power of God in my world. The more I pray, the more I will come to recognize sin and grace in my life—not because I have looked more deeply into myself, but because I have seen my life in relationship to the wider view of my world.

My view of life is like a view of a large valley from a mountaintop. From my position I can survey life, ministry, church, society, individuals. I make judgments about what has been and what could be. I make plans about my personal intrusion and insertion into life. I see where I've been and make plans about where I am going.

My theological and spiritual tradition has placed me on one of the mountains which surround the valley. When I reflect on life—my own life and life as experienced by my sisters and brothers—I climb that mountain and look at my wanderings through life. From my theological and spiritual mountain, I interpret the meaning of my activities in life and of other events in life. I gain perspective from the mountain.

Part of my reflection should be to recognize the shape and terrain of my mountain. I am, as a matter of fact, getting my view of life, of society, of church, of ministry, of individuals—even of myself—from this perspective. My reflection should lead me to recognize the perspective I am seeing from. How do I see life? Why do I see it the way I do? Why have I come to this promontory to gain a perspective on life? There are, after all, other mountains surrounding the valley.

What if I climb the mountain and from that viewpoint come to an awareness of all the immense suffering and the many injustices in our world? If I reflect on the reality of that injustice, and if I decide to take steps to seek justice and follow after it, what attitudes form in me? When I return to my concerns and activities in life, what do I do? How do I respond to those who are treated unjustly? How do I respond to those who oppress others? What do I say to my colleagues who claim also to be committed to the pursuit of justice? In short, what stance do I take toward my world and my ministry?

I can feel very much like a prophet, or like a liberator of people. I can even feel like a messiah. I can feel helpless —as if I, too, am oppressed. I can reject and despise the oppressors, and speak harsh words. Or I can become a reconcilor and try to open the eyes of those who are blind to what they do to others.

All these stances may be valid when I come down the mountain. But I shall return again and again to my elevated position of reflection, in order to gain perspective and direction in life. There I pray sincerely for the coming of God's Kingdom before I return again to the valley to work to make that prayer come true. Then I return again to the peak to view my life in the world.

If my praying is to be fruitful, I believe that I have to survey the land from some theological or spiritual mountain —and I have to do so regularly. But part of this reflection should examine the shape and terrain of my own mountain, my own perspective. Why have I come here? Is this where I am supposed to stand to view life? Am I being led to change my position? Would the kingdom of God be more fully established in our world if I contemplated less on my activity in the valley, and more on my reasons for climbing this particular hill? Am I being called to take a different perspective and attitude toward life? To change my outlook? To change my heart? To repent and convert?

I may climb my mountain of reflection and return to the valley again and again. I may even say some profound things and be driven by the passion in my heart, but my commentaries on the world below are shallow until I know which mountain I have climbed in order to survey the land

. . . until I know why I have chosen that particular mountain as my perspective. Have I been led to this mountain? Or have I selected it as my viewpoint for selfish and sinful motives?

There *are* other mountains. I don't want ever to pretend that mine is the only one—or even that mine is the only one for me. For now, it is enough to know that I am on my mountain because I have been led here. I may be led to view the valley from other perspectives at other times. I may be invited to do so by others who have seen the valley from other mountains and want to share with me what they've seen. There are other mountains for other people, and perhaps for me at other times. What is important is that I go where I am led by God.

Jesus himself was once led to a very high mountain by the devil and asked to survey the land from the perspective of achieving power and success in his mission. "All this I will give you if you fall down and do me homage." But Jesus knew he was not led there by God and he refused to see life the way he was invited to see it. "You shall do homage to the Lord your God; him alone shall you adore." He saw the valley below and recognized the perspective from which he was being invited to view that valley. He knew he had not been led there by God, so he knew he was not seeing the valley in the right way.

In my theological reflection on life I occasionally have to take my eyes off the valley and off the mountains and look to the sky, to the God who overhangs both the mountains and the valley. I have to allow my heart to speak whatever is in it: complaint, regret, elation, contentment, embarrassment, turmoil, adoration—whatever is there. I should remain with this prayer of my heart as long as I can, without trying to prolong it unduly.

I noticed that day in the mountains with my seminarian friends that the roads and trails which were so clear from the mountaintop were difficult to recognize when we later walked them. I tried to recall what I had seen from the top, but the trail and the rocks and the brush occupied more of my attention.

A view from the top gives perspective, but a guide is needed for walking the trails and taking the paths which have been planned. A view from above is necessary, but a companion in the valley is also required—something or someone to assure me that I am walking the way I planned and approved from the mountain perspective.

The Holy Spirit has been given to us as a guide.

In writing to the church in Galatia, Paul explained very simply and directly how Christians could know whether they were walking through life under the direction of the Spirit of God, or under the influence of self-indulgence and evil. He gave them a way of discerning which things were of God and which were not of God. He gave them a way of knowing whether they were being led through the valley of life by the Spirit of God, the spirit of self-indulgence, or the spirit of evil.

If the spirit of evil or of self-indulgence is at work in us as we find our way around the valley of life, the results are obvious: lewd conduct, impurity, sexual irresponsibility, idolatry, sorcery, hostilities, bickering, jealousy, outbursts of rage, selfish rivalries, dissensions, factions, envy, drunkenness, orgies and similar things. If these things are present in our walking and dealings in the valley, it makes very little difference how exalted our view from the mountain may be; we have lost our way!

Paul then tells the people in Galatia what it feels like to be led by the Spirit of God: love, joy, peace, patience, goodness, kindness, trustfulness, consideration for others and self-control. If these are what I experience as I wind my way through the valley of life, I can know that I am being led by the Spirit of God.

This Spirit of God is my companion as I trek up the mountain to reflect on life and as I walk along the paths of life trying to carry out the vision I received on the mountain. This Spirit is within.

Paul wrote another such set of criteria for knowing which spirit leads us in his first letter to the church in Corinth. In that letter he told the Christians what love looks like:

> Love is patient; love is kind. Love is not jealous; it does not put on airs; it is not snobbish. Love is never rude; it is not self-seeking; it is not prone to anger; neither does it brood over injuries. Love does not rejoice in what is wrong but rejoices with the truth. There is no limit to love's forbearance, to its trust, its hope, its power to endure.

If, as a result of surveying the land and of walking in the valley, we find in ourselves the things Paul speaks of in this letter, we can know that we are being led by the Spirit of God.

There is, however, only One who sees life right. There is only One who surveys the land with a perfectly clear eye. That One is represented by the sky. He alone knows how to view life correctly—the good and the bad, the sorrowful and the joyful, the just and the unjust. He alone knows how one ought to walk in the valley. He has sent his Son to this earth, who tells and shows us how to live in the valley and how to climb the mountain to which his Father leads us.

The gospel is my clearest map of life in this world, my surest guide to know if I am climbing the right mountain to get my view of life. If I want to know how I ought to walk the valley and what mountain I am to climb to gain perspective on life, my best guide is the gospel. There I see how Jesus walked and how he thought, and I can set out to do the same. He is God—the sky overarching mountains and the valleys, and yet he has come to earth to walk its terrain as I do.

A week after my hiking in the mountains of Colorado I was in Montana to do some interviews. I spoke with some old friends and met some new ones. On Sunday afternoon a group decided to take me to Tongue River Canyon, Wyoming. It was a most pleasant day of climbing the walls of the canyon on the trails. That night I wrote to God in my green book:

> Another glorious day of hiking in the mountains. Again, I have no beautiful and religiously expressive thoughts about it; it was simply a good and God-filled experience.
> I'm just very satisfied with life tonight. My body is more tired than my mind for a change. Really no thoughts on today, except that it was relaxing and renewing to hike around the canyon. I'll remember today as a holy day, made such not by our proclaiming it to be, or by our words or thoughts; it was holy because you made it and everything we touched today. It has worked its wonder in my body and my spirit. And I can't even sort out what that wonder is, let alone articulate it. But you are praised for Brother Mountain and Sister Stream and all who play there.

I still remember that day in the canyon of the Big Horn Mountains and the day a week earlier in the Rockies. When I got home, all I talked about was my two days in the mountains. As I talked, I knew I wasn't able to say what those days really meant to me. My words didn't capture the experience.

Several days later, while sitting all alone late at night, I remembered. And I wrote again in the green book.

> I saw an eagle. Can you believe it, I saw an eagle! I don't know why I think of it tonight. And I don't know why that's important to me. But in that canyon on Sunday I saw an eagle. It was so far above the walls of the canyon that that's the

only way I *knew* it was an eagle. No other creature could fly that high.

Never will I have to wonder why the Cheyenne see in the eagle a symbol of the Great Spirit. It was there in the blue sky where no one but an eagle could be. It was where I can never be, and yet it invites me to let my own spirit soar. God, I thank you for that single eagle. "Eye has not seen, nor has ear heard; nor has it entered into the human heart to conceive what you have in store for those who love you."

My spirit wants to burst out of my body with all I've experienced these past weeks. I'm in pain having to contain all the love and awe that's within me. I really feel like I could explode. And if exploding is what is in store for me, what I feel right now is the threshold of eternal happiness!

It's a very emotional moment, and I know it will pass . . . but thank you for it. Thank you for that eagle, and for these tears. Maybe I'm just going crazy, but such happiness and such fullness I don't ever remember before. You are blessed forever; especially for your generosity toward those who don't have the wings to fly to where you are. You come to us, and in the confined space of our spirits you take up residence.

Only a glimpse did I get. It was too high to do any more than recognize it. And at the time it was a novel thing. Now, only, does it seem to have meaning, and that meaning fills me. The mountains on the previous Saturday, the canyon on Sunday a week later, and the eagle soaring above all my experiences. I simply bow in worship of you who are symbolized by that eagle, so far above my most ecstatic experience, and yet come to earth to be with me. May you be blessed for your greatness and for your love for those who cannot be in your realm.

I saw an eagle, and I thank you. It flies above everything, but it makes its nest in the very

     cliffs I climbed. It's beyond me, but it's with me,
     and that is my God.

It was a beautiful moment whose meaning is only now unfolding for me. God is the sky. I had learned that earlier in a clearing between an orchard and a woods. The eagle is God come to earth—Jesus. Only God overarches all the mountains and the valleys and the plains. Only he sees aright. The eagle soars above all my experience of mountains and valleys and plains. But, like me, he nests in the cliffs. The God who is sky and his Son who is the eagle have sent their Spirit into my heart to be my companion so I, too, can walk in the valley, survive on the plains, climb the mountain to survey the land.

    If you would pray, climb the mountain, survey your land. From your height of reflection, cast your gaze not only on the land below, but also to the sky. And remember the eagle! It is of earth, but it assures us that what is of earth can have a view from the sky.

    If you would pray, survey the land.

Epilogue

In writing these words, I hope I've encouraged you to make space to hear him knocking and to make symbols to allow him entrance. I hope I've encouraged you to grasp the symbols of your own theological and religious and spiritual tradition. And beyond these, I hope I've enticed you to make symbols of your own.

Prayer is pleasant, logical, satisfying, profound . . . and it makes good sense. But I don't always experience it that way. If what I've written leads you to believe that prayer is all those proper things, without helping you to know that it is also unpleasant, confusing, frustrating, ordinary . . . and makes no sense at all, then I've failed to do what I wanted most to do.

Prayer is messy. Most grown-ups don't enjoy getting involved in messy things. Children do. They can be dedicated to the serious business of playing around in a mess, be it mud or sand, or dirt, or finger paint or jelly and peanut butter. We teach them eventually to be more proper, but part of their experience of having life begin to make sense is to be allowed the freedom to make a mess and to play in it. The child in each of us needs at times to be allowed the same freedom—to play around in the mess—in order to experience the reign and rule of God in our lives. It was, don't you know, over a "mess" that the Spirit of God first moved to bring about creation.

And finally, may I add again a word of caution. God is not your symbols; he is beyond them. So don't make your symbols your God.

And don't ever ridicule the symbols of others. We're all unique and, if we will open the door, he will come in to each of us just as we are. It's not up to any one of us to determine what it takes for any others of us to get that door open.

He does knock; make space to hear him. He will come in; make symbols that open the door for him.